The Inscrutable Japanese

装幀 ● 菊地信義
装画 ● 野村俊夫

翻訳 ● ジム・ラティマー／ルーシー・ノース

挿画 ● サトウ サンペイ（朝日新聞社刊「フジ三太郎」，新潮社刊「ドタンバのマナー」より）

DTPオペレーション ● ポイントライン

Published by Kodansha International Ltd.,
17-14 Otowa 1-chome, Bunkyo-ku, Tokyo 112.
No part of this publication may be reproduced
in any form or by any means without permission
in writing from the publisher.
Copyright © 1997 Kodansha International Ltd.
All rights reserved. Printed in Japan.

First Edition 1997
97 98 99 00   10 9 8 7 6 5 4 3 2 1

ISBN4-7700-2129-1

誤解される日本人
外国人がとまどう41の疑問
The Inscrutable Japanese

メリディアン・リソーシス・アソシエイツ[編]

賀川洋[著]

"Most of the world's troubles are brought about not by scheming and ill will but by misunderstanding and laziness."

Goethe
The Sorrows of Young Werther

世の中のいざこざの因になるのは、奸策や悪意よりも、むしろ誤解や怠慢だね。

ゲーテ
「若きウェルテルの悩み」

まえがき

日本はなぜ誤解されるのか。わかりやすく言ってしまえば、日本と外国とでは文化が違うからでしょう。しかし、多くの人は思います。どこの国だって独自な文化があるわけで、なぜ日本だけが特別に誤解されるのだろうと。

世界中には国の数だけ、そして民族の数だけ異なった文化があり、それぞれの環境のもとで風習や行動様式や思考方法が培われてきたことは理屈では理解できます。しかし、実際に他の地域からやってきた人と出会ったとき、その人の態度や行為とその文化背景とが、どう関係しているのかというメカニズムについては、わからないことだらけです。おまけに、得てして人は人を瞬時に判断してしまうため、さらに誤解が広がるのです。

日本は大陸国家でもなければ、一時期を除いて、世界中と広範に交わりダイナミックに歴史を変えてきた経験が希薄な国でもあります。しかし、現在はそんな日本に世界がくっつき混ざりあおうとしています。

どんな国でも、固有の文化が外から強く影響を受けるとき、摩擦が起り、誤解が拡大します。現在は、日本にとって特にそうした時期に当たるのでしょう。

だから、日本だけが特別に誤解されているかのようにも見えるのかもしれません。しかし、日本人はこれからはこうした軋轢を受け入れ、乗り越え、世界と共に歩まなければなりません。でなければ日本はますますかたくなに孤立してゆくでしょう。

本書では、日本人がどんな時に誤解を受けるのか、その

PREFACE

Why does Japan get misunderstood? A simple explanation would be because of its cultural differences. But since every country can lay claim to a unique culture, why, many people wonder, is Japan misunderstood so much more than other nations of the world?

That there are as many different cultures as there are nations and races in the world, and that different customs, behaviors, and patterns of thought have evolved in each of these environments is easy to understand on a theoretical level. But when one encounters a person from another country in real life, trying to see how that person's attitudes and behavior relate to his or her cultural background is an activity that is fraught with difficulties. And because of the human tendency to make instantaneous judgments of others, there is ample opportunity for misinterpretations to arise.

Japan is not part of a continent, and neither (with the exception of a few brief periods) does it have much experience of dynamic interaction with other countries of the world on a large scale. However, today Japan is linked irreversibly with the other nations of the world, and its culture and society is becoming affected by them.

Any country with a particular culture that receives strong influence or pressure from outside will inevitably have to suffer friction and misunderstandings will inevitably arise. And this is just what Japan is going through at the present time. This is what gives rise to the impression that Japan is particularly misunderstood by other countries. From now on, however, Japan must take the discord created by the influx of outside influences in its stride, in order to get along harmoniously with other nations in the world. To refuse to do so will simply mean that Japan will continue in stubborn isolation.

This book describes the mechanisms operating behind Japan-

メカニズムについて解説します。そして日本人の行動様式や文化背景をどのように外国に紹介すればよいかというヒントも提供します。

　外国の人が、日本人とつきあって不思議がり、怪訝に思い、残念なことに怒りを覚えたりしたときに、いかに日本のことを説明し、彼等の誤解をとけばよいのでしょう。また、外国人はいかに日本のことを理解して、心の準備をし、行動様式を変えてゆけばよいのでしょう。今、日本に必要なことは語り合う場を持つことです。そんな語り合いの準備、そして語り合いそのものの道具として、本書を利用していただければ幸いです。

　ただ、本書を外国人への言い訳には使わないでください。

「文化の違いからくる誤解はお互い50%ずつ責任があるのですよ。でも元々お互いに良い意思を持っていたはずです。その意思を尊重するためにも、ここで文化背景の違いについて理解し、お互いにどうアプローチすれば良いか考えましょう」

　このように語りかけ、日本からのメッセージを伝えましょう。本書がそんな本音の国際交流のために役立っていただければ幸いです。

ese behavior in instances where misunderstandings with other cultures occur. It also provides hints on how to explain Japanese behavior, as well as the cultural background behind such behavior, to people from other nations.

When foreigners sense strangeness in their interactions with Japanese, or grow suspicious and then, regrettably, angry, it is useful to know how to explain aspects of Japan that might help to straighten out their misconceptions. It is also useful to know how to get people from other countries to develop some sympathy for Japan, prepare themselves mentally for interaction with Japanese people, and adapt their own behavior accordingly. What is needed in Japan today is the opportunity for both sides to relate their positions to each other. I hope that this book can be used as a preparation and indeed as a means for people to carry out such mutual relating.

However, I do not want the observations in this book to be used as ways to excuse Japan to people from other nations.

"When misunderstanding due to cultural differences arise, responsibility usually lies 50/50 with each side. But the original intention was probably good on both sides. In order to respect the good intentions we both have, we should consider how best to approach each other, trying our very best to understand the differences in our cultural backgrounds."

Let us convey a message of mutual respect and shared responsibility from Japan. I would be delighted if this book can play a role in promoting real international exchange from the heart.

目 次

CONTENTS

第三章 • 日本の職場のミステリー

CHAPTER 3 • Mysteries of the Japanese Workplace

第四章・不思議な日本の社会現象

CHAPTER 4 • **Strange Japanese Social Phenomena**

曖昧な日本人

•

CHAPTER 1
The Ambiguous Japanese

1 なぜ日本人は相手の目を見ないの？

よく、日本人は話をするときに相手の目を見つめない国民だといわれます。確かに、外国、特にアメリカ人などと比較すると、日本人は視線を交わすことなくコミュニケーションをすることが多いようです。日本人は、相手を強く見つめることは、何か失礼な、相手を威嚇する挑戦的な行為であると考えるようです。親が子供を叱るときも、子供が親の目を見つめていると「何だそんな目をして」と、注意します。だから、日本では叱られているとき、子供はよくうつむいているのです。

逆に、アメリカでは怒られている時に子供がうつむいていると、「何で私の目を見ないんだ」といって親は注意します。

アメリカでは、相手の目を見ずに話を聞くと、その人はその話に興味がないのではないかと思われてしまいます。また、その人が何となく自信のない人に思え、最悪の場合は、何かやましいことがあったり、隠し事をしているのではないかと誤解されてしまいます。

ですから、日本人は例えどんなに英語ができても、この視線の問題で誤解を受けてしまうことがあるのです。

では、なぜ日本人は強いアイコンタクトを避けるのでしょう。そのヒントは、封建時代の日本にあります。130年前に日本が世界に向けて扉を開き近代化に着手するまで、日本の社会には厳然とした身分制度が存在していました。特に1600年から1867年までの江戸時代は、この制度が社会の隅々まで厳しくいきわたり、サムライなど身分の高い人と、一般の人々とは、結婚はおろか、話をすることも自由にできませんでした。特に、身分の高い人の目を見るこ

Why won't Japanese look me in the eye?

It has been said that Japanese avoid making direct eye contact during conversations. When compared to other nationalities, especially Americans, this is probably true. Japanese tend to feel that eye contact is rude and signifies an attempt to intimidate or challenge the other person. If a Japanese child looks a parent in the eye when he or she is scolded, the parent will berate the child for that, saying, "Why are you looking at me that way?" Consequently, most children learn to keep their heads down in front of an angry parent.

In America, avoidance of eye contact is taken as indicating disinterest in what is being said. At worst, it is seen as a sign of lack of self-confidence. Sometimes it can even be viewed as showing that the listener is hiding something or engaged in something immoral. If an American child looks down when scolded, the parent will say, "Look at me when I'm talking to you!"

Given these differences, even Japanese who speak English fluently may still invite misunderstanding due to lack of eye contact.

Why do Japanese avoid eye contact? One answer may lie in Japan's feudal history. Until just 130 years ago, when it opened its doors to the outside world and began to modernize, Japan had a strict class system. Every aspect of Japanese society was affected by this system, which reached its height during the Edo period (1600–1867). Commoners were forbidden to speak or have contact with the samurai warrior class, and inter-

とは大変無礼な作法とされ、時には死に値することもあっ
たのです。

　もちろん、そうした身分制度は、江戸時代が終わるとな
くなりましたが、この身分制度が日本人に与えた心理的な
影響は今でも残っているのです。ですから日本人は知らず
知らずのうちに、アイコンタクトを控えるようになり、同
時にそれは丁寧で作法にかなった行為でもあったのです。
　さて、アメリカはどうでしょう。アメリカの子供は、個
人の意見が大変尊重される民主主義の社会の中で成長して
いきます。強い視線こそが、自分の主張を裏付ける自信の
証、そして相手に対する信頼の証であり、伝統的にも良い
こととされています。
　もしそんな常識にのっとってアメリカ人が、強く日本人
を見つめて話そうとすると、日本人は困ったように視線を
逸らすかもしれません。また、人によっては、あたかも独
り言を言っているかのように、どこか別の所を見て話をす
る日本人もいることでしょう。その方が、日本人にとって
は心地よいのです。
　従って、特に顧客などと話をするときは、少し視線を弱
くした方が、相手もリラックスでき、商談がうまく進んだ
り、逆に相手の信頼を勝ち得ることがあるのです。

marriage was quite unthinkable. Not only was eye contact with a person of higher social status considered very rude, it could cost the offender his life.

Although this system ended with the Edo Period itself, its psychological and emotional impact on the Japanese psyche remains. Japanese still unconsciously avoid making eye contact as a way of being polite.

What about Americans? American children are raised in a society with democratic ideals, where individual opinions are greatly valued. Direct eye contact is seen as proof of self-confidence and trustworthiness, and has traditionally been a good thing.

However, when an American makes eye contact with a Japanese, there is a good possibility that the Japanese will be uncomfortable or embarrassed and look away during conversation. Some Japanese focus in the distance when speaking, as if talking to themselves. This is what is most comfortable for them.

Therefore, Americans would be well advised to limit their direct eye contact when speaking to Japanese clients. This will help the client relax and trust them, and business will proceed more smoothly.

② なぜ日本人は「YES」とばかりいうの?

さて、弱い視線の次に外国人が戸惑うのが、日本人がどんなことにでも「イエス」と答えてしまうことです。これでは、日本側にいわんとする意図が伝わっているのかどうか、外国人の方では判断できなくなってしまいます。

日本人は、「イエス」を「はい」と翻訳します。「はい」は肯定の意味と共に、自分が話を聞いているというサインを相手に送るときにも使用されます。ですから外国の人が話しているときも、日本人は曖昧な表現を使う代わりに、つい「イエス」と言ってしまうのです。

このように日本人が「はい」の代用として、「イエス」を多用してしまうとき、問題が起こるのです。なぜなら「はい」は様々な状況で使用できますし、意味もいろいろにとれますが、英語の「イエス」は、もっと意味が限定されているからです。だから、日本人がただ「イエス」というかわりに「Uh-huh」とか「I see」あるいは「Hmm」などと状況に合った信号を相手に送れば、そうした誤解も幾分緩和されるはずです。

さらに、日本人には相手が何か話をしているとき、その話を遮って、分からないことを確認したり質問したりすることを嫌う文化があります。相手の話を遮ることを、日本人は「話の腰を折る」といい、人の話は最後まで聞くものだと親は子供に教えます。最後まで聞いて、それで分からないことがあれば後で質問をするというのが、日本流の会話のマナーなのです。

もちろん、日本人が英語を聞くとき、分からないことは山ほどあるはずです。ところが、人の話を途中で遮ることは失礼だと思っている日本人は、分からない箇所があっても、「イエス、イエス」と言いながら、会話を進めてしまうのです。

2 Why do Japanese say "yes" all the time?

Westerners are often confused by the Japanese use of "yes" in English conversation. "Yes" seems to be said so often, it becomes hard to judge whether the Japanese has really understood what has been said or not.

In Japanese, "yes" is "*hai*." It signifies affirmation, but it is also a signal that the listener is paying attention to the speaker. When conversing in English, Japanese people will frequently interject the word "yes" while somebody is speaking, to convey that they are paying attention.

However, the problem is that while "*hai*" has room for ambiguity and can be used in many situations, the English "yes" is much less ambiguous. Therefore, if Japanese vary their responses according to the situation, with "Uh-huh," "I see" or "Hmm," instead of automatically saying "yes," the possibility of misunderstandings arising should be somewhat decreased.

Japanese dislike stopping someone in conversation to ask questions or to ascertain meaning. Parents teach their children to listen to a person until he or she has finished speaking. Interrupting someone in mid-speech is called "breaking the conversation's back." In Japan, one listens until the speaker is finished and then asks questions.

During English conversation, even if something is unclear, Japanese may move the conversation along by saying "yes, yes" because he or she assumes that interrupting the speaker would be rude.

　英語の世界、特にアメリカ英語の世界では、分からない箇所があれば、その場で相手の会話を止めてチェックしたり質問したりする習慣があるものですから、日本人がそれをしないと、アメリカ人は「この人は分かっているんだな」と思って、どんどん会話を進めてゆきます。すると日本人は、ますます分からない箇所が累積して、質問すらできないほど混乱してしまうのです。しかも、あまり分からなすぎると、それを相手にまた質問することもはばかられるものですから、最後にアメリカ人が「お分かりですか」と念を押しても、ついつい「イエス」といって、その場を凌いでしまいます。実は、そのとき日本人は、アメリカ人の言ったことの3割も理解していないのです。

　そこで、いざ仕事になると、日本人がすでに説明した内容を再び質問するなど、すべてがちぐはぐで物事が進展しなくなるのです。

　「日本人はイエスといっても、本当にイエスとは思っていない」という日本人への否定的なコメントは、実はこんな単純なメカニズムの違いから発生しているのです。さて、どうしたらこの行き違いを解決できるのでしょうか。日本人としては、言っていることが分からないときは、躊躇せずに相手の話を止めて質問する習慣をつけ、安易に「イエス」で逃げてしまわないよう訓練することが大切です。

　そして、相手にゆっくりと英語を話すように、複雑な単語や、俗語等の表現を使わないようにお願いするのもいい考えです。というのも、アメリカ人には、人にゆっくりと話をすることは、あたかも子供に話しかけているみたいで聞き手に失礼だという観念があり、会話のスピードを落とすことには抵抗があるのです。ですから、ゆっくり話してくれる方がありがたいのです、と説明すれば、アメリカ人は安心して協力してくれるはずです。

　また、込み入った会話の時には、重要なポイントを書い

In the English-speaking world in general, and the American English-speaking world in particular, the listener interrupts the speaker and asks for clarification when needed. So when a listener does not interrupt, the American assumes he is understood and simply continues talking. The Japanese listener, however, may well be having difficulty—and points that are unclear may accumulate to the degree that it becomes impossible to ask questions. When the American finally asks "Do you understand?" at the end of the conversation, the Japanese may well say "yes"—even though he has probably grasped only 30% of what was said.

It is not uncommon for work projects to get held up by these type of communication problems, or because Japanese ask about details that have already been explained.

This simple difference in listening style gives rise to the criticism that "Japanese say 'yes' when they don't really mean it." How can this problem be solved? If Japanese do not understand, they should avoid saying "yes," and not hesitate to interrupt a discussion and ask for clarification.

Japanese would also be well advised to ask Americans to speak slowly and to avoid difficult words and slang. Americans believe that speaking slowly to an adult is condescending, and they want to avoid seeming impolite or insulting. But if Japanese explain that they're comfortable with slow enunciation, Americans will happily comply .

It is a good idea to get down the main points of a

てもらうとか、分からない単語があれば、簡単な表現で繰り返してもらったり、スペルを聞いたりして確認するように努めたいものです。大切なことは、分からないときは最後まで待たないで、その場で話を止めてチェックすることです。そうすれば、アメリカ人も「ああ、この人は私の言っていることを聞いているな」と思い、より親切に積極的に話をしてくれるでしょう。

complex discussion in writing. You can also ask the speaker to repeat his ideas in a simpler way, or to spell out words you don't understand. The important thing is to clarify things by interrupting rather than waiting until the conversation is over. As long as an American knows you are listening to what he's saying, he or she will make an effort to help you understand.

❸ なぜ日本人は「メイビー」が好きなの?

　欧米人の間では、日本人はなかなか「ノー」と言わない、と信じられているようですが、本当はそうではないのです。日本人はちゃんとノーと言っているつもりなのですが、それがどうも彼らには理解してもらえないのです。はっきりと「ノー」というなんて失礼だと日本人は思っていますから、間接的に伝えようとします。でも外国人にはその微妙なニュアンスを感じとることができません。

　外国人が日本人からよく聞く英語の一つに「メイビー」があります。なぜ日本人は「メイビー」がそんなに好きなのでしょう。それは日本人からみると、「メイビー」は大変便利な言葉だからです。

　日本の社会では、はっきりと相手の意見を否定することは、タブーと言ってもよいほどにまずいことです。上司から部下に、あるいは友人同士の間柄では、こうしたタブーはあまりありませんが、ビジネス上の関係、さらには上の立場の人に対しては、「ノー」ということのタブーを常に考えておかなければなりません。

　というのも、伝統的に、日本人は人間関係の中では対立を好まない傾向があり、どうしても対立しなければならないときは、間接的な表現で、あるいは大変柔らかい表現でそれを相手に伝える風習が根付いているのです。

　この風習は、長い間日本人の間で培われてきたものですから、とても外国人には理解し難いものといえましょう。さらに、日本では、意見そのものと、その意見を言っている人の人格とを同一視する傾向があるため、相手に反論すると、その人の人格に攻撃をしかけているかのように誤解される恐れがあるのです。

　こうした背景から、日本人は、ときには「メイビー」ということによって、曖昧に「ノー」を表現しようとするのです。

3 Why do Japanese like the word "maybe"?

There is a common belief among Westerners that Japanese can't say "no," but this is not really the case. They do say "no." It's just that Westerners often don't understand it. Japanese consider it rude to say "no" directly, so it tends to be said indirectly. The problem is that many Westerners are insensitive to these subtle nuances.

One English expression commonly favored by Japanese is the word "maybe." Why is this the case? For them, "maybe" is a very convenient word.

In Japan, there is a strong taboo against directly refuting or saying something negative about someone else's ideas. While it may be tolerated among close friends or from superior to subordinate, it is still considered inappropriate to disagree with one's superior or business associates.

Traditionally, Japanese have a tendency to avoid confrontation. When absolutely necessary, however, they use indirect expressions and try to communicate their disagreement as mildly as possible.

This is sometimes difficult for foreigners to understand. Also, since Japanese tend not to distinguish between the opinion and the person stating it, there is a danger that the speaker may feel personally attacked if the listener disagrees.

Therefore, Japanese often express "no" ambiguously with "maybe."

　これに対して、アメリカでは、意見とその人の人格とを切り離して考え、あたかもキャッチボールをするように対立する意見でもどんどんお互いに投げ合います。だから、「ノー」といっても、それがそのまま相手の人格を攻撃していることにはならないのです。
「メイビー」と共に日本人がよく使う表現に、「I think it is difficult 難しいと思います」といった表現もあります。これを聞いたアメリカ人は、「そうか、難しいのは分かった。ではどうしたら可能性が広がるのか考えよう」と思い、さらに日本人に質問をします。しかし、この場合も日本人は間接的に「ノー」と言っている場合が多いのです。

　アメリカ人にとって、いかにして、日本人の「ノー」を理解するか。確かにこれは至難の技です。解決策としては、日本人のボディー・ランゲージを覚え、そこから言外の意味を理解できるようになることも一案です。しかし、それにもまして大切なことは、できるだけ個人的に親しくなることでしょう。ビジネスアワーを離れた個人的な時間では、日本人は意外と心を開き、率直な意見を話すものです。こうすれば、より日本人の本音に接することができるようになるはずです。

In contrast, Americans are more likely to view what a person says as distinct from who he is. They exchange opposing opinions objectively, as if tossing a ball back and forth. A direct refutation or contradiction is not usually taken as a personal affront.

Another English expression favored by Japanese is "Hmmm, I think it is difficult." An American hearing this probably thinks, "Okay, I understand it's difficult for him, but let's see how we can expand the possibilities," and continues working on the problem. In such a situation, however, the Japanese is probably saying "no" in an indirect way.

How can an American tell when a Japanese means "no"? Certainly, it is an acquired skill. One way is to pay attention to body language and other non-verbal communication. An even more important way is for business partners to get to know each other after work in social settings, where Japanese will feel freer to express honest opinions. If you do this, it will be possible to discover what they really feel.

4 なぜ日本人はくっつきたがらないの?

　ロシアでは、政治家同士が頬をすり合わせて挨拶するの
をよく見かけます。また、アラビア人同士は、ほとんど顔
をくっつけるようにして話をしています。では、日本人は
どうでしょうか。日本人はある程度相手との物理的な距離
を保って話をするようです。

　このように、人と人との心地良いとされる距離感は、国
や文化によって違いがあり、ここから思わぬ誤解が生まれ
ることがあります。ある程度の距離を必要とする日本人が、
日本とは異なる文化背景をもった人と話をする場合、その
距離を保とうとするがために、どんどん後ずさりをしてし
まうのです。相手が後ずさりをすれば、その人は自分を避
けているんだという誤解を生むことになりかねません。

　あるアメリカ人が、「私はこの前日本人と立食パーティ
ーで出会ったが、どうも相手に嫌われたみたいだ」とこぼ
していました。よく聞いてみると、話をしている間中、日
本人は後ずさりを繰り返し、おまけにまっすぐ人の目も見
ず、すべての返事が「メイビー」で、本当にこちらの意図が
伝わったのかどうかも分からなかったとのこと。

　このように、文化の背景には様々な相違があるものです
から、そうした事柄がすべて裏目にでると、このアメリカ
人のような誤解をしてしまうわけです。

　ロシア人やイタリア人、あるいは中南米の人ほどではな
いにしろ、アメリカ人はどちらかというと日本人より短い
距離で人と接することを心地良しとします。最近、若い世
代ではかなり変わってきてはいますが、それでも同僚同士、
または恋人同士、夫婦間であっても、日本人はアメリカ人
より距離を保って話をすることが多いようです。日本人か
らしてみれば、この距離感の違いによって、アメリカ人か
ら思わぬ圧迫感を感じ、何か自分が脅かされているかのよ

4 Why do Japanese avoid touching each other in public?

In Russia, politicians touch cheeks when greeting each other. When Arabs talk, their faces almost touch. Japanese, however, prefer to keep some physical distance when having a conversation.

There are cultural differences about what is considered a comfortable distance between people, and misunderstandings can arise. Japanese require a degree of distance. When speaking with someone from another culture, they often end up stepping backward in order to maintain this distance. Inevitably, the other person assumes that the Japanese is trying to avoid him.

One American grumbled, "I met a Japanese fellow at a buffet, but he didn't seem to like me." Listening closely to the American's story, it turned out that the Japanese kept moving away from him and avoided eye contact. He also said "maybe" to everything. The American couldn't tell if he was getting his point across.

These kinds of misunderstandings are a result of subtle cultural differences.

Americans are comfortable with a closer distance than Japanese, but they do not get as close as Russians and Italians. Latin Americans keep less distance than them. Recently, younger Japanese have grown accustomed to standing closer when talking. But in general, business associates, as well as couples (in public) and housewives, keep a greater physical distance when talking than Americans. Japanese tend to feel pressed or

うな錯覚に陥ってしまうのです。

　次に、この距離感と似たような概念に、会話における「間」の問題があります。日本人は会話にも距離感を保つことを心地良しとします。相手が何か話をすると、その話が終わって少し「間」をおいて自分の意見を相手に伝えたり、自分の話をしたりするのです。

　この沈黙もアメリカ人を大変心配させてしまうのです。アメリカ人の会話法は、テニスのボレーのようで、会話と会話の間にほとんど間をおかず、常に何かの音で埋めようとします。

　アメリカ人は特に沈黙に弱いようです。そのため、アメリカ人が日本人の前でプレゼンテーションを行い、質疑応答の時間になっても日本人が沈黙しているので、ああ、これは失敗だったと失望してしまうケースも多いのです。そう、もう少し沈黙に慣れ、黙って待っていれば、やがてパラパラと質問が出はじめて、最後にはちゃんとした反応を得ることができるのですが……。

「いや、皮肉な話だが、日本人がアメリカ人との交渉で優位に立てる武器。これこそが沈黙という武器なんだよ。じっと黙っていられると、アメリカ人はいても立ってもいられなくなるからね」とあるアメリカ人のビジネス・コンサルタントは言っています。そう、沈黙に強くなって、距離感に慣れることは、日本人とより親密に交流するための第一歩といっても過言ではないでしょう。

threatened when standing close in conversation due to a different level of comfort with physical proximity.

Conversation intervals also pose a problem. In addition to keeping a comfortable physical distance, Japanese are also comfortable maintaining intervals of silence in a conversation. When one person finishes a sentence, Japanese like to leave a short interval of silence before the next person begins conveying his ideas or telling a story.

This silence bothers Americans, whose conversations have much fewer intervals. They tend to fill in any absence of sound with words, like hitting a tennis ball back and forth.

Americans give the impression of being poor at tolerating silence. When Americans make business presentations in front of Japanese, they often feel they are unsuccessful because the Japanese don't say anything during the question and answer period. However, if they tolerate the silence and wait a while, there is every likelihood that the questions will begin and they will get good feed-back.

Some American business consultants say "It's ironic, but Japanese have a great weapon when negotiating with Americans: the weapon of silence. Americans can't stand it when Japanese don't say anything." It is probably not an exaggeration to say that the first step towards closer interaction with Japanese is to be more tolerant of silence and to get used to their sense of distance.

5 **なぜくっつきたがらない日本人が
通勤電車では平気なの?**

　それでは、なぜそんなにスペースを大切にする日本人が、
あのぎゅうぎゅう詰めの通勤電車に文句を言わないのでし
ょうか。

　もちろん、日本人も文句は言っています。誰もが平気で
あの電車に乗っているわけではありません。電車のドアが
開くと、皆争うように席を取ろうとしている光景をみれば、
日本人だってゆっくりと腰掛けて通勤したいのだというこ
とは容易に理解できます。

　以前、日本のある放送局が面白い実験をしていました。
朝の通勤電車にぎゅうぎゅうに押し込められている人々を
集めて、喫茶店に招待し、しばらくお茶を飲みながら会話
をしてもらったのです。その後、その人たちに再び満員電
車に乗ってもらいました。すると、今まで平気で体をくっ
つけていた人同士が、今度はお互いを意識し、必死で距離
を保とうとしたのです。つまり、見知らぬ人同士では無頓
着に押し合っていた人々が、知り合いになったら距離感を
やたらと気にするようになったわけです。

　日本人は知人とそうでない人を区別し、いったん知り合
いになると様々なマナーを通して、相手に気を使おうと努
力するようです。反面、この実験からもお分かりのように、
人間関係のない見知らぬ人のことは、あまり気にしないよ
うです。

　たしかに、日本語で見知らぬ人を意味する「他人」という
言葉には、どこか冷たい響きがあります。英語に「他人」に
あたる単語があるかどうか疑問ですね。

　問題は、外国人は「他人」の中でも、最も遠くにいる「他

How can Japanese who don't like physical contact in public not mind the trains?

If Japanese value their space so much, why don't they complain about their jam-packed commuter trains?

Certainly, some people do complain. No one could ride those trains without minding the crush. The sight of all those people rushing for seats as soon as the train doors open makes it easy to understand how even Japanese want to relax and sit down during their commute.

A Japanese TV station once did an interesting experiment. They invited a group of people who had been packed together in a morning commuter train to a café, and encouraged them to chat casually over tea. After that, they put them back on to a crowded train. The same people who previously hadn't minded physical contact with each other now became very self-conscious, and tried desperately to maintain distance from each other. People who had indifferently pushed and shoved each other as strangers suddenly became concerned about their physical proximity once they became acquainted.

It appears that Japanese make a strong differentiation between acquaintances and strangers. Once they become acquainted, they make an effort to look out for each other. On the other hand, as this experiment makes clear, Japanese care less about people with whom they have no relationship.

This is further evidenced by the harsh-sounding Japanese word "*tanin*," which means "other person" or "stranger," but also has the implication of "outsider."

Consider the unfortunate fact that foreigners tend to

人」とみなされていることです。実際に、外国人の中には、長期間日本に滞在しても、入国してから帰国するまでずっと「他人」として疎外され、日本の社会に溶け込めないまま日本を離れてしまう人もかなりいます。とはいっても、ビジネスでも個人の生活でも日本人と付き合うためには、自分が日本人にとって「他人」でなくなるよう努力しなければならないのですから、外国人も大変です。ある意味で、この外国人を「他人」として取り扱うものの見方は、日本が世界と交流してゆくことを妨げている考え方ともいえるのではないでしょうか。

be viewed as the most extreme form of "*tanin*." Some foreigners remain "*tanin*" from the minute they come to Japan till the minute they leave, even if they have stayed for a long time. They never manage to enter real Japanese society. In order for foreigners to have deeper relationships in business and private life, they have to transcend the status of "*tanin*," which is often very difficult. Actually, the tendency to treat foreigners as "*tanin*" in Japan is one factor that impedes truly international communication.

6 なぜあんなに気を使う日本人が、
外国を旅行するときは態度を変えるの?

　さらに日本人の「他人」という考え方を理解するために、もう一つの日本特有の概念を紹介しましょう。それは、「内と外」という考え方です。

　「内」とは、社会のサークルの内側、すなわち知人同士の間柄を、「外」とはその外にいる他人を意味します。「内」の輪は、状況によって大きくなったり小さくなったりします。例えば、会社の同僚は「内」ですが、会社以外の人は「外」の人です。ところが、その会社が関係している顧客や購入先、あるいは同業者であってもお互いに交流があるような場合は、そうしたすべてが「内」となり、それ以外の人たちは「外」として扱われたりします。

　外国と対応するときは、多くの場合、日本全体が「内」で、外国は「外」と考えられます。現に外国や外国人（スラングでは外人ともいいます）という言葉自体が、「外」の漢字を使用していることからも、その事は理解できるはずです。

　問題は、日本人は「内」に対して大変気を使いますが、「外」のことにはあまり関心を払わない傾向があることです。ある意味で、「内」に十分気を使うには、「外」の利益を無視しなければならないこともあるわけで、そうしたことから、「内」を重んずれば重んずるほど、「外」に対して無理解になってしまうのです。

　外国を旅行する日本人の団体が、レストランで他人の迷惑も考えずに大声で話したり、あたり構わず写真をとったりすることは、そうした日本人の心理と大きく関係しているといえましょう。

　彼らにとって、「内」とはその団体旅行のグループです。そして彼らは「外」である外国に来ているわけですから、他

6 Why are normally considerate Japanese inconsiderate when traveling abroad?

In order to understand the Japanese concept of "*tanin*," it is important to understand the Japanese concepts of "*uchi*" and "*soto*."

"*Uchi*" refers to one's inner social circle. "*Soto*" refers to those people outside that inner circle. The "*uchi*" circle gets larger or smaller depending upon the situation. For example, colleagues in the same company are "*uchi*" but anybody outside the company is "*soto*." Customers or suppliers connected to the company through interaction become "*uchi*," while all others are treated as "*soto*."

In most interactions with foreigners, Japanese consider themselves "*uchi*" and foreigners "*soto*." This is underlined by the words "*gaikoku*" and "*gaikokujin*" (or "*gaijin*"), which are constructed with the kanji character for "*soto*."

Unfortunately, Japanese tend to pay a lot of attention to "*uchi*," but they pay much less attention to "*soto*." In some ways, paying too much attention to "*uchi*" causes one to ignore the benefits of "*soto*." The more one gives priority to "*uchi*" the more insensitive to "*soto*" one becomes.

It's probably true to say that the behavior of Japanese tour groups abroad—careless that they're bothering others by talking loudly or taking pictures everywhere, even in restaurants—has its basis in this particular psychology.

For the Japanese tour group, the travel group is "*uchi*" while the foreign country is "*soto*." Although usually

人からどのように思われるのか、気にはするのでしょうが、鈍感になってしまうのです。

確かに、グローバルな時代と言われる現在、この「内と外」という考え方は、日本にとってマイナスです。日本人自身がこの「内と外」のメカニズムについて反省し、もっと積極的に世界と交流してゆかなければなりません。

しかし、日本人にとって、それがプラスに働いていることもあるのです。例えば、ビジネスの関係で「内」の中に入ってしまえば、少々無理を言っても相手はこちらのいうことを聞いてくれますし、特別な配慮やサービスをしてくれます。

一度この人は「内」だと認識されれば、無言の信頼感の中でお互いに助け合い、協力し合ってゆくことができるのです。

だから、外国人だって、自分が外の人だとばかり考えて、被害妄想に陥っていると、そうした利益を享受できないまま日本を去ることになってしまうのです。

もちろん、ビジネスを、そして人間関係を造ってゆく中で、外国人が「内」の人間として認められる可能性がないわけではありません。それには、良い日本人の知人の紹介を受けて「内」の輪へと通じるドアを叩くことが必要です。また、「ギブ・アンド・テイク」を繰り返すことによって「内」へと導かれる過程も知っておくとよいでしょう。すなわち、ビジネスはビジネスと割り切らずに、相手の状況を理解し、その個人と親しくなることが大切なのです。

日本でうまくやってゆくためには、日本人の行動をよく観察し、どのように人を迎え、エンターテインし、そして人を「内」に入れているかを知る必要があります。それは結構忍耐と努力を要するでしょう。しかし、そうした努力をする人のことを日本人は尊敬するのです。そして、一度、

careful about what others think of them, the people in these groups end up behaving in a rude, insensitive way.

In this global age, the "*uchi/soto*" mindset is a minus for Japan. Japanese themselves should reflect on the "*uchi/soto*" mechanism and engage more evenly with the world.

There is also, however, a plus side of this mindset. For example, once on the inside of a business relationship, a person will be listened to even if he or she asks a big favor. Somebody on the "inside" will get special consideration and service.

Once a person is recognized as being "*uchi*" there is mutual cooperation and aid within a context of unspoken trust.

Foreigners in Japan may be conscious of being treated as outsiders and feel victimized as a result. They often end up leaving Japan unable to enjoy the benefits of being an insider.

However, there are ways for foreigners to be seen as insiders in the context of doing business and forging relationships. One way to gain access to the inside is through the introduction of a good Japanese friend. It is also possible to gain access by a repeated process of "give and take." It important not to view business just as business, but to understand the circumstances of your associates and make an effort to get to know them as individuals.

To do well in Japan foreigners should observe the behavior of Japanese. Learn how they greet people and entertain them and bring them into their inner circles. This requires a lot of patience, but Japanese respect those who make this kind of effort. Foreigners can build

日本側の尊敬を獲得できれば、外国人でも日本人と同じように、親密なビジネス関係を構築することができるのです。

close business relationships once they gain respect from
the Japanese side.

7 なぜ日本人は面と向かってものを言わないの?

「人を介して」という表現を日本人はよく使います。人が
何か間違いをした場合、日本人の同僚はそれに気づいても、
その場で直接注意しないかもしれません。時には、友人や
知人を通して、すなわち「人を介して」注意をすることもあ
るでしょう。

このことにアメリカ人はうんざりしてしまいます。「何
で直接私に言わないのだろうか。そんなに私のことが嫌い
で信用していないのか」とアメリカ人は思うかもしれませ
ん。あるいは「何てかげでこそこそと動く奴なんだ」と怒り
を覚えるかもしれません。

しかし、多くの場合、その日本人は問題を起こした相手
に気を使って、穏やかにメッセージを伝えようとしている
だけなのです。ではなぜ、日本人はそのようなことをする
のでしょう。日本人は伝統的に人と対立することを好まな
いということは、すでに別の場所で説明しました。「和」を
もってことに臨むという考え方から、日本人は様々なコミ
ュニケーションの方法を独自に編み出してきたのです。

もし、誰かの問題点を直接指摘したら、いったいその人
はどう思うだろうかと日本人は考えるのです。摩擦が起き
るかもしれません。しかし、もし人を介して話してもらえ
ば、メッセージの内容も柔らかくなるし、直接の摩擦も避
けられます。そこで、第三者を介する方法を選ぶのです。
するとアメリカ人は、「摩擦だってそれが建設的であれば、
大いに結構。人を介して言われると何かそいつのことが信
じられなくなってしまう」と反論するかもしれません。

しかし、実は日本人には日本人なりの建設的な摩擦の解
決方法があるのです。それは、人を介してメッセージを受

7 Why won't Japanese speak to me directly?

In Japan, when someone makes a mistake, his colleagues often refrain from correcting him directly—even though they may be aware of it. Instead, they alert him to his mistake through a friend or acquaintance. This method is reflected in the expression "through others" which Japanese often use.

This irritates Americans, who often wonder, "Why won't they speak to me directly? Does he dislike me or distrust me?" Or they may be offended and think, "What a back-handed person!"

In most cases, the Japanese does care about the other person, and is trying to convey the message gently. But why do Japanese resort to this kind of behavior? As we have seen, Japanese have had a tradition of avoiding confrontation where possible. As a result of this, a variety of communication approaches have developed with the objective of maintaining harmony, or "*wa.*"

Japanese worry that if they point out someone's mistake directly, misunderstandings could arise and produce conflict. If the message is delivered through someone else, however, its effect will be softened and conflict avoided. Thus the help of a third party is preferred. By contrast, an American usually welcomes constructive conflict, and if he is told about a problem through a third party, he will not necessarily trust the conveyer of the message.

Japanese have their own constructive way of resolving conflicts. Once the person has received the message via a

けた後、ちょっと時間をおいて、改めてその人と食事をしたり、時にはお酒を飲んだりして、楽しい雰囲気の中で一度起こった摩擦や誤解を解き合って、より建設的な人間関係をつくるのです。そうすれば、十分にお互いに時間をかけて考えることによって、時には怒りを沈めながら、いろいろと振り返り、お互いを理解する下地を造り、すべてが「和」を保った形でリスクもなく解決できると考えるのです。

「ああ、まどろっこしい」と思うでしょう。より直截なコミュニケーションを好む、あるいは必要ならば対立もよしとするアメリカ人からみると、確かに、この複雑で長いプロセスにはうんざりとさせられるかもしれません。でも、伝統的に「和」の概念を最も基本的で大切な概念だと思ってきた日本人にとっては、これは最良の方法なのです。しかし、その同じ方法が、文化の違うアメリカ人には「スニーキー」で「相手を信じていない行為」ととられてしまうわけです。
　確かに何事に関しても、日本人は婉曲を良しとします。直接本人に話をするときでも、日本人は問題の箇所を指摘するのではなく、その周辺の事柄をそれとなく伝えることで、相手に本意を伝えようと努力するのです。これを無視して、はっきりとものを言えば、人のことを考えない、子供っぽい行為として軽蔑されかねません。これは、対立することにより、お互いの立場を明確にし、その上で是非をはっきりさせようとするアメリカ人にとっては、最もなじめない習慣なのかもしれません。

third party, in a while he will often be invited out to eat and drink with the concerned party. A warmer, more congenial atmosphere will be achieved between them. This way, a more constructive relationship is built, and previous conflict or misunderstanding resolved. This allows for time to revisit various issues and to create a basis for understanding while passions are cooling off. In Japan, conflicts are usually resolved without risk by working towards maintaining a sense of harmony or "*wa.*"

This can be frustrating to Americans, who tend to prefer direct communication, and even confrontation when necessary. They may be irritated by the long and complicated process of Japanese conflict resolution, but for people who traditionally accept "*wa*" as the most basic and important aspect of their social structure this is the best method. It is often considered by Americans as evidence of "sneaky" or "untrustworthy" behavior, however.

In Japan, the best way in most situations is usually the indirect way. Even in face-to-face situations, Japanese won't go directly to the main point. Instead, they try to convey their true intent indirectly. If you ignore this custom and are too direct in your needs and assertions, you run the risk of being considered childish or insensitive. You may even be viewed with contempt or hatred. For Americans, who prefer clarity and a confrontational style, this is probably the most difficult Japanese custom to accept.

8 なぜ日本人は謝ってばかりいるの?

　なぜ、日本人は「和」の精神を大切にするのでしょうか。
おそらくそれは、今でこそ、日本は産業や商業の発達した
国というイメージが定着しているようですが、元々は農業
を基本とした、せまい土地を耕す村社会として発展してき
た国だからです。

　限られた土地を耕し、田圃をつくり、米を育てるには、
村のみんながお互いに協力し合い、今日はある村人の田植
えを手伝い、明日はその隣の人を手伝ってというふうに集
団で活動をしてゆかなければなりません。

　しかも、日本は、カリフォルニア州とさほど変わらない
広さの土地に、アメリカの全人口の半分が生活する混雑し
た国なのです。

　その結果、広大な大地を一人で開拓しなければならなか
ったアメリカとも、狩猟によって生活を立てていた北方ア
ジアやヨーロッパの人々とも違った価値観が日本人の間に
培われていったのです。集団の和を保ち、そのためならば、
個人の要求や欲望をも制限することが良い価値観として評
価されるようになったのです。だからこそ個人主義という
日本語には、どちらかというと否定的なニュアンスがあり、
日本人は個人主義は利己主義と似た価値観と誤解している
こともあるようです。

　日本人は、相手に対しへりくだった対応をとることが美
徳だと考えています。問題が起きれば、あるいは相手に何
かお願いすることがあるときは、日本人はよく、「すみま
せん」とか、「申し訳ありません」という「I am sorry」と翻
訳される表現を使い、相手との話し合いをはじめます。こ
う言うことが、日本人にとっては、その場をなごませて相
手と交流を進める基本的なマナーなのです。だから、多く

Why do Japanese apologize so much?

Why do Japanese place such a high value on "*wa*"?

Modern Japan's image is that of a highly industrialized capitalist nation, but historically its society was agricultural and village-based, with people cultivating tiny plots of land side by side. Cooperation in the village was essential in order to construct rice paddies, grow the rice, and cultivate the limited available land. One day one villager would need help planting rice, and the next day his neighbor would need his help in return. It was necessary to operate as a group.

Furthermore, Japan is a crowded country whose entire population is half that of the U.S. squeezed into a land mass about the size of California.

Different values were fostered from those of Americans, who could claim a large piece of land for themselves, or from Europeans or Northern Asians, who hunted animals for survival. In Japan, maintaining group harmony and restricting individual demands and desires were highly regarded. This explains why individualism has a negative connotation there, and can sometimes be interpreted as simple egoism.

Among Japanese, a display of modesty is considered a sign of virtue. When people have a problem or need to ask a favor, they frequently begin the conversation or discussion with phrases such as, "*sumimasen*" or "*mōshiwake arimasen*," both of which can be translated as "I'm sorry." These expressions ease and prepare the atmosphere and promote interaction. Foreigners are

の外国人は、何で日本人は謝ってばかりいるんだろうと首を傾げてしまうのです。アメリカ人からみると、謝ることは自分が間違っていたことを相手に表明することで、極端な場合は相手の軍門に降ることを意味してしまいます。

　従って、日本人からすると、アメリカ人はなかなか謝らず、逆に何を言っても自己を正当化するようなことばかり返ってくるような気になるのです。日本人は、極端に言えば天気が悪くても、自分とはまったく関係のないことで相手が困っていても、「申し訳ありません」と言ってから会話にはいります。

　ですから、日本人が「I am sorry」とか「I apologize」と言ったとしても、それは必ずしも日本人が自らの非を認めているわけではないということを知っておく必要があります。これは「まず謝ってから本題に入る」というプロセスなのです。このことを知らないがために、日本人との交渉が暗礁に乗り上げてしまったケースはいくらでもあります。というのも、日本人は謝った後、なかなか妥協してこないことがあるからです。

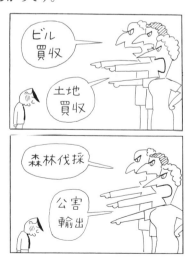

often puzzled by why Japanese apologize so much. From an American point of view, apologizing means you've made a mistake. In extreme cases it means defeat.

Japanese, on the other hand, feel that Americans rarely apologize and that they always justify themselves, even when they are wrong. Apologizing is very basic for Japanese. Sometimes they begin a conversation by apologizing for the bad weather, or for the problems another person may be having.

It may be good to realize that Japanese are not necessarily admitting fault when they say "I am sorry" or "I apologize." An apology is simply a way of starting the process of getting to the main discussion topic. If people don't know this, negotiations with Japanese can become deadlocked, because an apology doesn't necessarily indicate a readiness to compromise or to give in.

9 なぜ日本人は自分の正当性を主張できないの?

　日本では、上司から注意をされたり、顧客からクレームを受けたりしても、例え、それが自分のせいで起きた問題ではなくても、まず「ごめんなさい」と一言謝り、あまり相手の指摘に対して反論はしないものです。日本では、即座に反論したりすると、かえってその人の人格に疑問をもたれてしまうリスクがあります。

　即座に反論して「和」を乱すより、そこはまず謝って、別の機会に、あるいは別の場所で、必要ならば説明をするという方法を多くの人はとるのです。その場で言い返せば、「ああ、この人はすぐに言い訳をする、心の狭い人だ」と思われてしまうからです。

　日本人とアメリカ人が共に働いている職場で、「アメリカ人に何か一言いうと、10も20も言い訳がかえってくる。だから、もう話をするのが面倒になってね」と日本人が言っていたのを聞いたことがあります。しかし、アメリカ人は、必要ならば自己の正当性を主張するのは人間として当然の権利だと信じていますから、自らの行動が責められるべきではないと感じれば、それを説明しようとするのは当たり前のことなのです。これが日本人の目には、無駄な自己プロモーションのように映ってしまいます。長期にわたる人間関係が基本となっている日本では、人と人の間には長く続いた信頼関係がすでにできあがっています。ですから、たとえ相手の不平や文句に納得がいかないとしても、即座に自己の正当性を主張して火に油を注いでしまう結果になるよりも、その場はとりあえず引き下がる方がよいのです。

　加えて、日本人には「間」の感覚があることを思い出しましょう。どのような会話でも、特に対立するような内容を

9 **Why can't Japanese insist that they are right?**

Japanese who are dealing with superiors or customers usually don't argue with what someone says to them. Rather, they say *"gomen nasai"* ("I'm sorry") when they get a warning from their boss or receive a complaint from a client, even if they are not at fault. In Japan, if you argue back at someone, you run the risk of it being taken as a character assault.

Most people choose to apologize first, instead of arguing back and being antagonistic. If necessary, they explain things at a later opportunity. If you argue back at that moment, the person will think, "Oh, he's a narrow-minded person who makes excuses."

I once heard this comment from a Japanese who works with Americans: "Dealing with Americans is so difficult. They've got ten to twenty excuses for anything I point out to them." Americans believe it is a natural human right to justify themselves if necessary. They see nothing wrong with explaining or defending their actions if they feel they are not to blame. From a Japanese perspective, however, such behavior is inappropriate self-promotion. In a context where long-term relationships are the norm, there is a basic sense of continuity and trust between people. Even when one side has a complaint that the other feels is unjustified, it is far better to let the truth come out later than to fuel an argument by defending oneself on the spot.

In addition, remember the Japanese sense of *"ma"* or interval. It's important to take plenty of time before

含む場合は、十分に「間」をもって話をすることが大切です。即座に反論するのは、どのような場合でもマイナスになってしまうのです。実は「間」とは、数秒から数分の間だけではありません。そこではいったん会話をおしまいにして、数日間、あるいは数週間「間」を置いた後に、再びその主題について話をすることもあるのです。

　それでは、その「間」の間に日本人は何をしているのでしょう？　その間に彼らはやはり「人を介して」相手に理解してもらうように調整したり、あるいは関係者といっしょに飲みに行って意見を交換し、コンセンサスをとったりしているのです。

　この非公式の調整活動が外国人には見えないものですから、「日本人は何か彼らだけでこそこそと話をして……」ということになってしまうのです。いずれにせよ、こうした調整のプロセスを踏んで、十分に「間」をおけば、主張したいことも、すでにその要点が相手に伝わっているわけですから、相手から見ても、それが「強い自己主張や言い訳」とは取られなくなるのです。

　メッセージを「間」をおいて柔らかくして相手に伝えることも、日本人の「和」を保つための大切なテクニックの一つなのです。

voicing opposition, no matter what the subject or situation. It is not good to quickly offer an opposing opinion. In reality, "*ma*" is not just a few seconds or minutes. Sometimes it can take several days or weeks to bring up the topic again after the initial conversation.

Just what are Japanese doing during this period of "*ma*"? They make adjustments, either by working through a third party to get themselves understood or by going out drinking with the parties involved to exchange ideas and build consensus.

Since this unofficial adjusting is done behind the scenes, Westerners think, "The Japanese must be hiding something, talking amongst themselves...." But if you take these steps and leave enough time to elapse, you will avoid giving the idea of being too self-justifying or making excuses. Your message will have already been conveyed.

Conveying a message indirectly through "*ma*" is an important technique by which Japanese maintain "*wa*."

10 なぜ日本人は曖昧なの？

「和」を尊ぶ日本人からみるならば、曖昧であることこそ知的であり、センスがあって、相手を思い相手と共存し、共に内部の人間同士として利益を享受するための武器なのです。曖昧であることで、要らぬ対立を避け、ことをスムーズにさせ、さらにチームワークを促進してだんだんとグループの中に溶け込めるようにするのです。

そして、その常識に「インディビジュアリズム」を良い価値観として共有してきたアメリカをはじめとした国の人々は、真っ向から挑戦します。アメリカ人にとって、曖昧であることは、論理的でなく、知的でないどころか、相手に対して大変失礼な行為となるのです。

このように、国や文化の違う人同士が交流するときに、自らの常識や価値観だけに頼って相手を判断してしまうことは大変危険なことなのです。そして前向きであった人でも、常識や価値観の違いに気付かず、自らの価値観だけに頼って相手を判断し続けると、ついには相手に対して後ろ向きになってしまうのです。

外国の直截で強いコミュニケーションのやり方に苦しめられている日本人は、まず自らを自らの価値観から解き放して、客観的に相手の文化を観察してみることが必要でしょう。もちろん、逆もまた真なりで、外国人も日本の文化背景を知ることによって、単に怒りを覚えて日本人の同僚の曖昧な態度を批判するという不幸を回避することができるはずです。そして、最初はぎこちないまでも、少しずつ相手の行動様式を真似てみて、お互いに調整をし合いながら、試行錯誤を繰り返すなかで誤解をといてゆけばよいのです。

もちろん、お互いの文化背景の相違について客観的に説

10 Why are Japanese so ambiguous?

In Japan, being ambiguous is intelligent and savvy. Ambiguity is a weapon which enables one to co-exist harmoniously with others and to enjoy the benefits of insider status. Ambiguity avoids or smooths over conflicts and promotes teamwork, allowing one to modestly blend into the group.

People from countries such as America who value strong individual self-expression pose a challenge to this commonsensical Japanese notion. For Americans, ambiguity is illogical, irrational, and even unintelligent. It can also be seen as very rude.

When people from different countries or cultural backgrounds interact, it is unwise to judge others only from the point of view of one's own common sense and values. However, even open-minded people often continue to judge others from one's own standpoint, without noticing differences in common sense and values. They wind up turning their backs on each other at the end of the day.

If Japanese are troubled by Americans who communicate strongly and directly, I suggest that they step back from their own values and observe the other culture objectively. The reverse holds true as well—foreigners can avoid angrily criticizing the ambiguous behavior of their Japanese colleagues by learning a little about their culture. Then, however awkward it may be, both sides should make efforts to adapt their ways of behaving. Through repeated trial and error misunderstandings can be resolved.

Of course, you won't have as much trouble to go

明してくれる友人や経験者がいれば、それにこしたことは
ありません。

　自分が不愉快だと思っているときは、往々にして相手も
同じように考えているわけですから、お互いに自分だけが
正しいと思いこまないように努めたいものです。

　そして、もう一つ、言葉さえ通じればすべては解決する
のにと思うことこそ、最も危険なアプローチだということ
を知っておきましょう。言葉の背景にある文化の違いを理
解せずに言葉だけ覚えても、かえって複雑な誤解を招くも
ととなりかねません。

through if you have an acquaintance of the other culture or someone knowledgeable who can explain differences to you objectively.

If you dislike what the other person is saying or doing, try not to conclude that you are the only one who is right, since the other person is probably feeling uneasy too.

One more thing. It's very unwise to think that everything can be resolved through words alone. Remembering the words but forgetting the cultural differences behind them invites all sorts of misunderstandings.

第2章

控えめでプライド高き日本人

●

CHAPTER 2
The Modest But
Proud Japanese

1 なぜ日本人の演説はわかりにくいの?

　日本人はなぜ単刀直入に物事の本題に入らないのかという疑問があります。実際日本人は、その事の成り立ちや背景を最初に理解してから、核心にアプローチしようとします。

　例えば、ある会社の概要について語るとき、まずその会社がどのような経緯で今に至ったかを説明し、次第に現在の業務内容、そして将来への展望といったような事柄へ話題を発展させてゆきます。

　よく日本人は未来よりも過去を大切にする国民であるといわれます。すなわち、先に物事の歴史を明快にすることにより、その事柄の価値を理解し、そこから未来を見ようとする傾向があるようです。例えば、昔はその人の出身がどこで、どのような身分だったのか、その家庭はどこまで歴史がさかのぼれるのかといったことが、その人の価値を見極める一つの手段でした。従って、物事の背景を語ってから本論に入るやり方は、日本人にとっては当然のことなのです。

　ところが、アメリカ人はその逆です。アメリカでは、昔からその人が今何ができるのかということが、その人の価値を決める要因でした。開拓者が木を伐採し、外敵から身を守るときに、いっしょに働く人の出身を気にしていても仕方がありません。今その人にどれだけ力があるかがその人を判断する大きな基準だったのです。

　ですから様々に異なった背景を持つ移民の国であるアメリカでは、まずは何をおいても明快なメッセージを強調することが説得術の基本となっていったのです。従ってアメリカではまず語りたいことのポイント、すなわち結論を最初に強調します。

Why are Japanese speeches hard to understand?

Why don't Japanese get to the point more quickly? Actually, they usually try to get to the core of the matter by first understanding the background and context of the problem.

For example, when giving an overview of a company, a Japanese will first explain how the business arrived at the present situation. Next, he will explain the company's current affairs and future outlook.

It is often said that Japanese value the past over the future. The worth of something is understood by first clarifying its history, and only then considering the future. For example, they might look at a person's background. What is his status? How far back does his family's history go? This is one method of determining a person's worth. Therefore, it seems natural for a Japanese to arrive at the main subject after putting it in context.

Americans tend to do the opposite. The criteria for evaluating a person's worth are based on merit. When settlers logged the native forests and defended themselves from attack, they didn't have the luxury of worrying about the background of the people they worked with, since they had no choice. The main standard for judging others was based on practical results.

America is a country of immigrants who come from very different backgrounds. The key to getting acceptance of one's views is the ability to persuade and state one's message clearly. Therefore, the main point or conclusion is emphasized at the beginning of a statement.

　まず語りたいことのポイントを話した後、それをサポートする理由を語り、そして例示を行い、さらに結びの形で、再度核となるメッセージを強調するというやり方が欧米では伝統的にとられてきました。だから、アメリカ人には、日本人の起承転結法が理解できません。起承転結とは、日本人が伝統的にスピーチや記述をするときに使用してきた論理展開法で、まず、ものごとの起こりと背景を述べ、別の事例を導入し、最後に結論を導き出すやり方です。ためしに日本のことを知らないアメリカ人に起承転結法で話をしたら、10人のうち、半数以上が結論を誤解してしまいました。

　とくに、結論が見えなくなった場合、アメリカ人は退屈したり、あるいは結論を確認しようとして会話の中に割り込んできたりするものですから、状況はますます悪くなるのです。そういうことがあると、日本人は再び背景から話をやり直しますから、より一層アメリカ人は退屈してしまうのです。

　だから、もしアメリカ人向けに日本式のスピーチを行うことがあれば、最後まで我慢して話を聞くように聞き手に頼んでみましょう。結論はきっと最後のほうに明快に見えてくるはずだからと。そして日本人は日本人で、できるだけ語りたいポイントを最初に話すように努めることです。

In the Western tradition, you state your main point, give supporting reasons and examples, and then re-state your core message in the conclusion. Americans are puzzled by the Japanese use of "*kishōtenketsu*," a style of logic used in speeches and in relating accounts. This style presents the background of the event and gives related examples, and only then comes to the main point, in the conclusion. In one test, ten Americans with no knowledge of Japan were spoken to in the "*kishōtenketsu*" style, and less than half understood the conclusion.

When the conclusion is not stated initially, things can go from bad to worse. Americans get bored or interrupt the speaker in anticipation of the conclusion. When this happens, Americans wind up even more frustrated, since the Japanese speaker usually just starts from the beginning again.

When a Japanese intends to give a speech to Americans in a more Japanese style, it is best to inform the listeners that they should listen patiently until the end, at which time the conclusion will become clear. Also, it may be a good idea for Japanese to indicate their main point at the beginning, if possible.

なぜ日本人は明快に表現しないの?

　日本人の言い方が具体性を欠いて、多分に雰囲気だけを伝えようとするために、外国からきた人を当惑させることがあります。

　例えば、日本人のボスが部下に「さあ、未来に向けて頑張ろう」と言います。言いたいことは何となく分かるのですが、外国人はそれに対して「いったい未来の何に向けて頑張るんですか」と質問するかもしれません。

　すると日本人は「何って分かってるだろう。会社の未来の繁栄のために頑張るんだ」と答えます。それでもメッセージは曖昧です。会社の未来のためにどのように頑張ればよいのか、さっぱり分からないのです。

　よく、日本人は言外の意味を込めて相手にメッセージを伝えるといわれます。すなわち、「一を聞いて十を知る」という諺があるように、もし日本人がメッセージを事細かに伝達すると、かえって押しつけがましく、相手を馬鹿にしているかのような印象を与えかねません。

　優秀な人ならば、一を聞いただけで十分かってくれるわけで、逆に上手な話し手は一で十を伝えるよう、含蓄ある表現でスピーチを行うと考えられているのです。

　さて、海外ではどうでしょう。多数の民族が混在して国を造ってきたアメリカや、常に国と国とが衝突し、民族が混ざり合ってきたヨーロッパなどでは、歴史的にもメッセージを明快に論理的に伝達しないと相手に大変な誤解を与えてしまうことが多々ありました。したがって、これらの国々では、十を伝えるには十をしっかりと伝達できる人が知的なスピーカーとされ、リーダーとしても尊敬されてきたのです。

Why can't Japanese explain things clearly?

Foreigners are often bewildered by the Japanese way of speaking, which conveys atmosphere but lacks concreteness.

For example, a Japanese boss may say to his subordinates, "Let's hang in there for the future!" What he is really saying is clear to his Japanese staff, but Westerners may wonder, "What exactly is he saying we should hang in there for?"

The Japanese would answer, "You should know what I'm talking about. We should all do our best for the company's future success." Even so, the message remains ambiguous. The foreigner still has no idea of the concrete measures he should take on behalf of the company.

It is often said that Japanese convey messages containing unspoken meanings. The proverb "Say one, know ten" illustrates the belief that if the whole message is given all at once, a person can give the impression of being too pushy or patronizing to the other party.

If the listener is smart and can grasp ten things when only one is spoken, it follows that a good speaker should use expressions with implied meanings. By saying one thing, ten things will be communicated.

In other countries such as America, which is a melting pot of many nationalities, and Europe, where countries battled each other and people of many nations were mixed together, history shows the consequences of misunderstandings. A message needs to be conveyed clearly and logically, and people who can communicate perfectly are respected as intelligent speakers and leaders.

　そうした文化背景を持つ外国人にしてみると、日本人の説明の仕方は往々にして不十分で、はっきりしません。そこで、例えばアメリカ人なら日本人に「WHY? なぜ」と質問します。すると、日本人は何か自分の説明に対して反論でもされているのではないかと思ってしまい、あわててしまうものですから、ますます曖昧な説明に終始してしまうのです。

　そして、まずいことに、日本側は一とはいわないまでも五ぐらい説明して、それで十分カバーしたつもりでいると、外国人は実際に全体の半分しか理解していないといったことが起こり得るのです。

　これでは、ビジネス上で重大な支障が生じかねません。言った言わないといった不愉快な言い争いが後で起きてしまうかもしれません。

　こうした誤解を防ぐためには、日本人は自らのメッセージに対して何度も「WHY?」と自問してみて、すべてを理解してもらえるまで、その内容を明確に伝えることが大切ですし、具体的にポイントを述べる努力をすべきです。

　そして、アメリカ人をはじめとした外国人が、すぐに「WHY?」と質問してくることへの心の準備もしておきましょう。

　また、双方とも、自らのボディー・ランゲージ、すなわちジェスチャーが相手にも伝わるものと過信しないことも大切です。よく、日本人は後頭部に手を置いて、うつむきながら歯の間から息を吸い込んで、「こりゃ大変だ」というようなメッセージを相手に伝えようとしますが、外国人からみれば、それはただ奇妙な動作に見えるだけで、いったいどのようなことを意味するのか見当がつきません。

　通常、メッセージは言葉とボディー・ランゲージが一緒になって、はじめて相手に伝わるものです。しかし、異文化間の交流では、その公式は必ずしも当てはまりません。控えめなジェスチャーをする日本人と、大きなジェスチャーを好むアメリカ人では、ボディー・ランゲージの表現法自体に差異があることを、常に頭に入れておく必要があるようです。

Foreigners who come from this cultural background feel that the way Japanese explain things is insufficient and confusing. An American will ask the Japanese "why?" and the Japanese explanation will simply get more and more ambiguous—because he thinks that the American is disagreeing with his explanation.

Unfortunately, there are cases in which a Japanese may explain five points to get ten across, thinking that this is enough. But the Westerner may still only understand half of his explanation.

Obviously, this leads to problems in business and may give rise to conflict. The American may complain, "No, what you said isn't what I heard."

To avoid misunderstandings like this, Japanese need to convey the content clearly until everything is understood. They should ask themselves "why" and make an effort to convey their points concretely.

Japanese should also prepare themselves to be asked "why?" by foreigners, particularly Americans.

Additionally, it's important for both parties to be aware of body language or gestures. When a Japanese puts his hand behind his head, or hangs his head and sucks air through his teeth, he is trying to communicate that the situation is difficult. The Westerner tends to view this as strange behavior and does not consider what it might mean.

Messages are usually given both verbally and through body language—but different cultures have different styles. Japanese gestures tend to be subtle, while Americans are more exaggerated. We should always keep this difference in mind.

3 なぜ日本人はいつもにやにやしているの?

　ボディー・ランゲージの中で、最も大切なものの一つが表情ではないでしょうか。共同でビジネスを成功へと導くには、互いの信頼が必要です。そんな時、表情は、ありのままの気持ちや考えを相手に伝え、信頼関係を築く上での重要な武器にもなり得るのです。

　そうした意味で日本人の表情を考えてみると、不可思議なことがたくさんあります。まず、すでに説明しましたように、日本人の視線は曖昧なため、いったい何を考えて話をしているのか、外国人には分からないことが多いのです。それだけでなく、外国人にしてみると、日本人の笑みそのものがよく分かりません。

　日本人はあまり自らのことを強く主張することによって、周囲との「和」を乱すことを恐れる国民性から、ついつい表情を和らげ相手に接しようとしてしまうのです。ですから日本人は辛い時や悲しい時でさえ、笑みを浮かべたりして、それが外国人にとっては不可解な笑みとうつり、誤解の原因となってしまうのでしょう。

　これはことアメリカ人に限らず、自らの感情を比較的オープンに表現することの好きなラテンアメリカやロシアなどといった国の人にとっても同じことで、悪くすると「この日本人は我々のことを侮辱しているぞ」と思われることもあるかもしれません。

　その上、日本人は手を上下させたり、体を動かしたりもあまりしませんね。悪いことに、どちらかというと、腕を組んだりといった、いわば閉じた動作を好むようです。しかも、人によっては会議中に目まで閉じたりして。

　腕を組んで目を閉じるということは、じっくりと物事を考えているということだとは、日本人の間だけで共有でき

3 Why do Japanese smile so often?

Facial expressions are one of the most important aspects of body language. Successful cooperation in joint business endeavors requires trust. Facial expressions convey honest and open feelings, and are a very important tool in establishing trust.

Japanese facial expressions can be mysterious. As we have seen, it is difficult for foreigners to tell what Japanese are thinking from the look in their eyes. This ambiguity is compounded by the Japanese smile itself.

Japanese are afraid to disturb the "*wa*" of those around them by expressing themselves too strongly. Therefore, they try to communicate subconsciously through mild or unemotive facial expressions. They may even smile when they are unhappy or in the midst of a tragic situation. Such incomprehensible smiles become sources of misunderstanding.

At worst, the foreigner may feel, "This Japanese is making a fool of me." This reaction is not limited to Americans. It is also felt among Latin Americans and Russians who like to express their feelings more openly.

Also, Japanese don't move their hands or bodies much, preferring closed body movements like folding their arms across their chests. Some even close their eyes during meetings.

Japanese interpret folded arms and closed eyes to mean the person is thinking carefully. But foreigners

るメッセージで、外国人からみれば、「この人眠っている
のかな」と思われても仕方がありません。

　アメリカでは、人と話をするときは笑みを浮かべて、で
きるだけ体を開いたオープンな姿勢で話をすることを良し
とします。何か考え事をしているときでも、あごに手を当
てたり、「うーん。そうだなあ」などという言葉を使って、
相手に自分が考えていることを伝達します。ただ黙って目
を閉じているだけでは、何のことか分からないのです。

　日本人は、まずは外国人と話すときには曖昧な笑みをや
めて、心の中と表情とを一致させる訓練をする必要があり
ます。嫌いなのか好きなのか、腹を立てているのか敬意を
表しているのか、あるいは同情しているのか心配している
のかなどといった状況を判断し、深刻な話題には深刻な顔
を、楽しい話題には楽しい顔をすることが大切です。また、
できるだけリラックスしたオープンな姿勢で相手に接する
ように努めましょう。

　そして、どちらかというと日本人より背も高く大柄で、
ジェスチャーも大きめな外国人の前でも、堂々と相手の目
を見て話をするよう心がけたいものです。豊かな表情と、
時には身振り手振りを普段よりも大きくして、全身で自己
を表現すれば、きっと彼らもあなたに好感を持って耳を傾
けてくれることでしょう。

can't be blamed for wondering if the person is sleeping.

When Americans speak, they think it's best to smile and speak with an open body posture. Even when considering something, they may put their hands on their chins and explain, "Well, what can I say..." as an indication that they are thinking. Therefore, it's hard for them to understand it when some one simply closes his eyes and says nothing.

When Japanese talk to foreigners, they should refrain from keeping a habitual smile, and practice expressing their feelings more in their facial expressions. They should also evaluate whether the other person likes or dislikes something, is angry or respectful, sympathetic or worried. It's important to have a serious face for something serious, and a happy face for something happy. Furthermore, try to keep a relaxed and open posture whenever possible.

Try to make direct eye contact and to speak with confidence—even in front of Westerners, who generally are much taller and bigger and use more exaggerated gestures. If you express yourself with hand gestures, body language, and emotive facial expressions, Westerners probably will respond and listen better to you when talking.

4　なぜ日本人は堅苦しい姿勢をしているの?

　アメリカ人が日本人と打ち合わせなどをしているとき、日本人の堅苦しい姿勢がとても気になることがあります。「あの人はあたかも肩にハンガーでもはいっているようだ。どうしてあんなにカチッとした姿勢をしているんだろう」

　これは日本人と商談をしたあるアメリカ人のコメントです。

　日本人は相手に対して敬意を表する場合、とくに姿勢に気を付けます。背筋を伸ばして、手を膝の上に置いて、必要なら丁寧に頷きながら人に対応します。顧客や地位の高い人、あるいは年長者といった、日本人からみると立場の上の人に対しては、とくにそうした姿勢で接することがマナーを心得た行為となるわけです。

　もちろん、アメリカにもマナーはあります。大切な顧客とはじめて出会ったときや、自分にとって重要な立場にある人と打ち合わせをするとき、話し方やもてなし方に気をつかうことは、アメリカでも正当なマナーとして尊重されています。

　しかし、その後でアメリカ人はできるだけ平等な土壌で話をしようという努力をします。例えば、上の立場の人が下の立場の人に「ファーストネーム」で呼んでくれと促して、そこからはお互いに打ち解けた会話をしようとしたりするのも、そうした努力のあらわれです。

　それに比べて、日本ではちょうど身分制度でもあるかのように、ものの言い方や姿勢、さらには車に同乗するときの座る位置にいたるまで暗黙のうちに決まっていて、その関係はよほどのことでもない限り変わることはありません。

　こうした上下関係に基づく姿勢や応対の方法は、お隣の

Why do Japanese have such rigid posture?

Americans are often irritated by the rigid body posture that Japanese adopt in conversation. "He looked as if he still had a coat hanger still in his jacket. Why is he so stiff?" commented an American about a Japanese businessman he had dealt with.

Japanese are particularly mindful of body language when showing respect. They sit up straight, place their hands on their knees and nod at appropriate intervals. This kind of posture is especially common in interaction with someone of a higher social position, such as a customer or an elderly person.

Of course, Americans have such manners as well. In America, treating someone politely through forms of speech or hospitality is considered appropriate and correct. This applies when initially meeting a valued customer or when talking with someone in an important position.

However, after the initial greeting, Americans make every effort to talk with the person on an equal footing. This is evidenced by the fact that the senior person urges the other to call him by his first name, encouraging a relaxed and more balanced conversation.

In Japan, however, it is extremely unlikely that social positions are forgotten in conversation. How one speaks, holds the body, and even where one sits when riding together in a car, is inherently set. It is almost as if a class system still existed.

In neighboring Korea, one can see a similar hierarchy-

韓国などでも似たようなものを見ることができますが、これらの作法は儒教道徳と深く関連したものといえそうです。2000年以上も昔に孔子によって説かれた儒教は、とくに封建時代には、この儒教の考え方を時の為政者（いせいしゃ）が奨励したために、日本や韓国では常識として、深く人々の間に根付いていったのです。儒教は社会の秩序を保つために、人の身分を尊重しようという考え方で、それがとくに日本をはじめとしたアジア諸国に大きな影響を与えました。

したがって、ほとんどの日本人は知らず知らずのうちにこうした伝統の影響のもとで、人と人との関係や、それに基づく作法や風習を習得し、法律の上ではすべての人が平等となった現代社会でもそうした基準をもって人に接しているのです。

そういうわけで、顧客である外国人がはるばる海の向こうからやってきた場合、あるいはその人が顧客ではないにしろ、わざわざ遠い外国から訪問してきた場合、日本人はホストとして敬意を表そうと、そうした堅苦しい姿勢をしてしまうのでしょう。

問題は、そうした姿勢をとり続けると、儒教的な背景を持たないアメリカ人のような外国人は、逆に型にはまった付き合いにくい人だと誤解してしまうことがあるということです。とくに最近のアメリカでは、ますます人と人とがカジュアルに、同じ立場で付き合うことを良しとするようになってきていますから、そうした誤解がなおさら起こりやすくなっているといえましょう。

based posture and interaction. These manners are deeply connected to Confucian morals and are over 2,000 years old. Confucian ways of thought were historically encouraged by the ruling class, especially in the feudal period, and became firmly established as common sense values in Japan and Korea. Confucian ideals emphasize the importance of hierarchy in maintaining social order, and still exert a major influence in Asian countries, especially Japan.

As it is, Japanese subconsciously acquired this traditional influence. Even in modern society, where people are equal under the law, Japanese relate to each other in manner and custom influenced by ancient Confucian standards.

Therefore, when a client has come all the way across the ocean, or even if he is not a customer but someone who has made the effort to pay a visit from a far away place, Japanese show them respect as a host and take on a rigid manner when meeting them.

If Japanese make no adjustment in this kind of attitude, however, those without a Confucian background could misjudge them as too stiff and distant. The likelihood of this misunderstanding is even greater with Americans, due to the growing trend of more casual and equal interaction.

5 なぜ日本人は自分のことを
馬鹿にしたような言い方をするの?

　上下関係を大切にする日本社会において、外国から来た
人が戸惑うことの一つに、日本人が極めて控えめに自己を
PRすることがあげられます。

　人と人との付き合いにおいて、常に自分を人の下におい
てへりくだったものの言い方をする人を、日本では謙虚な
人として尊敬します。それは不思議なことに、上の立場の
人にもいえることで、下の立場の人が敬意を表した場合、
それに応えるかのように相手に丁寧にできる人を日本人は
尊敬するのです。

　実際、日本では大会社の社長や、極めて著名な芸術家な
どが、講演などで「まだまだ勉強の最中で、こんな場所に
立つのはお恥ずかしいかぎりですが」と言って話をはじめ
たりすることもよくあります。

　日本には「能ある鷹は爪を隠す」という諺があります。こ
れは、能力のある人はそれを外に表さずにいるものだとい
う意味で、自分の能力を誇示しないことは、ある意味で人
との和を保ってグループの中で活動することを第一に考え
る日本人にとって、最も適した行動なのです。

　一つの例を紹介しますと、日本人は贈り物をするときに、
たいてい「つまらないものですが」という前置きをしてから
相手にそれを渡します。たとえ高価なものであっても、日
本人はへりくだってそのように言うのです。

　また、就職の面接などでは、「私はまだまだ未熟で何も
分かりませんが、どうぞよろしくご指導をいただきますよ
う」などといった言い方をする応募者をみかけます。

　それでは、同じようなことをアメリカの会社の就職の面
接で言ったらどうなるでしょう。「こいつはいったい何を
しに来たのだろう。悪い冗談でも言ってるんじゃないか」
と思われればまだ良い方で、「何も分からない人間がここ

5 Why do Japanese talk in a self-deprecating way?

In Japanese society, which values hierarchical relation-ships, one thing that confuses foreigners is the extreme-ly reserved way Japanese present themselves.

Japanese respect modesty. Someone who puts him-self below others and who speaks modestly is admired. Those in higher positions who respond politely when they are shown respect by their subordinates are admired. Ironically, the more accomplished someone is, the more modest he should be.

In fact, when presidents of large Japanese compa-nies or famous artists make speeches, they often begin with this comment: "I'm still learning and I'm embar-rassed to be standing here in front of you."

The Japanese proverb "The wise hawk hides his talons" signifies that clever people don't have to show off their cleverness. In a society where maintaining group harmony is a top priority, not showing off one's abilities is the most appropriate behavior.

For example, when Japanese give a gift, they usually say, "It's just a useless little thing." Even though the gift may be expensive, Japanese present it in a modest way.

Furthermore, when interviewing for a job, many applicants say, "I still have so much to learn. Please help me."

If the same thing was said in an interview at an American company, you can imagine what would hap-pen. The interviewers would ask themselves, "Why did he bother to come? This must be a bad joke." At worst,

に来てもしょうがないじゃないか」と即断されてしまうのではないでしょうか。

　確かに自己をしっかりとPRできることを良しとする文化背景を持つアメリカからみれば、この日本人の逆説的な自己PRの方法はどう考えても納得できないものかもしれませんし、こうしたプレゼンテーションを行ったばかりに日本人が誤解を受けたケースはいくつもあるのです。

　しかし、実はこうしたへりくだった言い方を通して、日本人はちゃんと自分の能力を相手に誇示しているのです。誰も「何もわかりませんが」という言葉をその通りには捉えません。そう言えば、相手は「なるほど、この人はなかなか仕事のできそうな人だな」と思うものなのです。

　逆に、「私はこんなにたくさんのことができます。どうですか」などといってPRをすれば、それは日本ではかえって不自然で、「この人は口だけの人で信用できない」という印象を与えかねません。したがって人と人との付き合いにおいても、へりくだり、「教えていただく」という姿勢をとれば、多くの人は心を開き、単に人間関係だけでなく、商談などもスムーズに展開してゆくものなのです。

　日本人が常に謝辞を述べる背景には、このへりくだった人間関係造りのテクニックがあるということも覚えておいてください。

he would be dismissed as "someone who knows nothing and lacks initiative."

Americans feel that the ability to promote oneself is a valuable skill. It would probably be difficult for many of them to accept the paradoxical Japanese style of self-promotion. There are a number of examples of Japanese who have given presentations this way and were completely misunderstood.

In reality, Japanese proudly display their ability by speaking with humility. No one interprets the words "I don't know anything" literally. If you speak in this way, people will think, "He seems like a competent worker."

Conversely, promoting yourself by saying how much you can accomplish is seen as unnatural. In fact, you run the risk of giving the impression that "This person is all talk and can't be trusted." If you are humble and ask "Please teach me," most Japanese will open up to you, and relationships and business negotiations will proceed more smoothly.

This Japanese tendency toward humility in building relationships also lies behind the tendency constantly to express appreciation.

6 **なぜ日本人は奥さんのことを誉めないの?**

　このようにへりくだったものの言い方をする日本人の社会では、自分の家族のことを人前で誉めることもあまり良いこととは思われていません。

　日本人はよく自分の子供のことを「愚息」と書いたり、あるいは奥さんのことを「愚妻」と表現したりします。もちろん、その人の子供も奥さんも愚か者ではないのですが。

　この「へりくだる」メカニズムをみてみると、面白いことに気づきます。すでに日本の社会での「内」と「外」との関係については説明しましたが、この「内」から「外」へ向かって自己を表現するときに、人々は特にへりくだった対応をするのです。

　従って、最も「内」の関係にある家族を「外」に紹介するときは、特に気を使って謙虚にものを言うわけです。同じことは、会社の同僚や部下を「外」に向かって紹介するときにも当てはまります。

　「田中はまだ若輩者で、社会のことを何も知りません。どうかよろしくご指導いただきたくお願い申し上げます」と、会社の上司が部下の田中さんを顧客に紹介することは、ごく当たり前のことで、このことは「内」の関係にある田中さんからみても、自分のことを侮辱していることにはならないのです。

　ですから、もし日本の家庭に招待されて、「今日は妻のまずい手料理でも」と言われても、外国人の皆さんはがっかりしないことです。その奥さんはきっと素晴らしい料理であなたをもてなしてくれるはずです。

　ところで、日本でも最近は、女性がどんどん社会に進出

6 Why do Japanese husbands avoid praising their wives?

In Japanese society, where humility is held in esteem, praising your family in front of others is not considered a positive thing.

Japanese men frequently call their sons and wives "stupid." Of course, this is not because they actually are stupid.

When you look at this mechanism of "putting oneself down," you notice something interesting. We've discussed the connection between "*uchi*" and "*soto*" in Japanese society, and here we see it in action. Japanese use humility and depracation when talking about members of their inner group to those on the outside.

When introducing one's family, those who are closest to you, take special care to be humble and depracating. The same approach applies to introducing colleagues and subordinates to outsiders.

For example, Tanaka's boss introduces him to clients by saying, "Tanaka is still immature and doesn't know anything about society. Please guide him."
This is very natural, and from Tanaka's point of view on the inside, not insulting at all.

Another example is when guests are invited to a Japanese home. The husband often says, "Please have some of my wife's terrible cooking," even though in reality the wife treats them to a delicious meal. Westerners may be disappointed or offended the first time they encounter such behavior.

While Japanese women are increasingly pursuing

するようになりました。しかし、それでも日本の多くの家庭では、妻の伝統的な役割はちゃんと残っているようです。妻は料理をして、夫のお客をもてなす役割を担うことが多く、そのためにせっかくお客さんがきても台所にひきこもったまま、お客と話をしたりという機会が少ないケースも多々あります。これは、家族全員でお客と交流することが常識であるアメリカからみれば、少々変に見えるかもしれません。

伝統的な日本の家庭では、妻は「奥様」といわれ、文字どおり家の奥で家のことを取り仕切る要の役割を果たす存在でした。

それは、女性を家庭の中に閉じこめることから、男女の平等という概念には反するものでしょう。しかし、反面それだけに「奥様」は、夫よりも子供の教育や家の財政などには発言権がある場合も多く、そうしたことから女性が、家庭に必要なものを購入するディシジョンメーカーであることも事実なのです。ですからもし女性にそっぽを向かれると、その製品は日本では売れなくなってしまいます。そんな女性の逆説的なパワーを理解することも、外国の企業が日本で成功する秘訣の一つといえましょう。

いずれにせよ、伝統的な「内」と「外」の考え方でみるならば、「奥様」とは最も「内」の社会である家族の、その最も「内」にいる存在です。だからこそ、なおさら夫は妻を大切にしながらも、外に向かって「愛妻」をへりくだって紹介するわけです。

大切であればあるほど、あるいは信頼関係があればあるほど、「外」に向かっては、外国人からみれば一見侮辱しているかのような表現で、その人を紹介するんだということを、外国から来た人は理解しておく必要があるでしょう。

もちろん日本人としては、こうした「へりくだった」アプローチが、外国ではともすると自分の思いとは逆にとられてしまうということを知っておいた方がいいでしょう。

their own careers, the wife's conventional role in the home still remains in many families. Therefore, the wife does her part in entertaining by preparing the meal. Because of this role, she is tied to the kitchen and often does not have the chance to talk with the guests. This seems strange to Americans, since for them it is natural for everyone to interact with the guests.

In traditional Japanese families, wives are called "*Okusama.*" As indicated by this name, literally "Mrs. Interior," wives play the role of managing household affairs from within the house.

This seems antithetical to the concept of male-female equality, since it implies that women are shut up inside the house. However, the wife has more power than the husband to decide the family's financial affairs and the children's' education. Women are also the decision-makers in purchasing household necessities. Consumer products that don't appeal to women don't sell. Understanding the paradoxical nature of Japanese women's economic power is one of the secrets of success for foreign companies.

According to the traditional social constructs of "*uchi*" and "*soto*," the wife occupies the innermost position in an intimate family. That is why the husband introduces his beloved wife in a depracating way to outsiders, even though in fact he cares deeply about her.

The more valuable a person is, the more trusting the relationship, the more he or she will be introduced with an expression which might appear humiliating to Westerners. People from outside Japan need to understand this.

At the same time, Japanese should be aware that this kind of depracating approach might be taken in the wrong way by foreigners.

7 **なぜ日本人は譲り合うの?**

　外国人からみれば控えめな態度が目立つ日本人ですが、そうした日本人を象徴する行為が「譲り合い」なのではないでしょうか。

　ビルやドアの前などで、日本人同士が相手を先に入れようとして、「どうぞどうぞ」「いえそちらこそ、どうぞ」などといってお互いに譲り合っている光景をよく目にします。

　また、夕方同僚や顧客とお酒を飲みに行くと、ビールの瓶を持ってまず相手のコップに「さあ、いきましょう。どうぞ」といってそれを注ぎ、その後で今度はそのビール瓶を受け取った相手が先にビールを注いでくれた人に注ぎ返したりしています。

　日本の居酒屋さんでは、ビールの瓶は大きくてコップは小さいことに気づきませんか。より相手に頻繁にビールを注げるようにという文化背景がそこに現れています。自分がもっとビールを飲みたいときも、まず相手に注ぐのです。すると、相手もこちらの控えめなメッセージに気がついて、すぐにビールを注ぎ返してくれるのです。これは、日本人の間では儀式にも似た当然のマナーで、それだけに外国で誰もが自分で自分のビールを注いでいる場にはじめて出くわして、多くの日本人はびっくりしてしまいます。

　さらに、典型的な例としては、お年寄りなどが道で出会って、お互いに何度もおじぎをしている場面です。欧米では一回の握手で挨拶が終わりますが、日本では一回の会話毎に相手に謝辞を送り、それの返答としてまた相手におじぎを返すというようなことが頻繁に行われます。

Why do Japanese yield to each other?

Many Japanese have a reserved attitude, which is probably best represented by their mutually yielding behavior.

Japanese can often be seen making polite concessions to one another. For example, often when entering a building or a room, they insist that the other person go first. "Please, please," one says. "No, you first. Go ahead," the other responds.

When Japanese have after-work drinks with colleagues or clients, they pick up the bottle and pour beer for the other person first. Then, that person pours beer in return for the first person, and so on.

Beer bottles in Japanese bars (*izakaya*) are big and glasses are small. Pouring beer frequently for others illustrates the Japanese cultural value of give-and-take. When you want more beer, first you should pour beer into your partner's glass. He will understand this subtle message and immediately pour beer for you. This is a natural ritual for Japanese. Most Japanese are surprised when they go abroad and see that everyone pours their own beer.

Another typical example of yielding is that of old people repeatedly bowing to each other in the street. In the West, greetings end with a single handshake. In Japan, it's common to offer appreciation, which will be met with a bow, at each part of the exchange, and to respond in kind. A conversation during a visit to someone's house might go like this:

「この度は本当にご迷惑をおかけして申し訳ありませんでした」
「いえ、こちらこそ何もお手伝いができませんで」

「何をおっしゃいますか。お礼の申し上げようもありません」
「そんな、ご丁寧に恐縮です。お恥ずかしいかぎりです」

　このような会話が繰り返され、なかなか前に進みません。

　これが欧米ですと、
「いや。先日はご招待いただき、ありがとうございます」
「どういたしまして、いらして戴いて感謝します」
　だけで終わってしまいます。日本ではこの二倍から三倍のやりとりを経ないと、会話が先に進まないのです。

　こうした風習の背景には、日本人のグループへの帰属意識がありそうです。グループでの調和を大切にするため、自らが突出することを日本人は余り好まないのです。ビールを相手に注ぐのと同じように、ビジネスの場では、まず相手の意見を聞いてから、それに対して控えめに自分のコメントをつけ加えます。
　また、相手側の意見に対して受け入れられない事柄があったりすると、まず間接的に、あるいは曖昧にお断りする前に、同席している同僚や上司、あるいは部下の顔をみて、「さあ、どうでしょうね」と意見を求めたりといった行為をします。

　しかし、この譲り合いにも限度がありますよね。よく世界で一大事が起きたときに、日本政府が「諸外国の対応を注目しながら政府としても対策を……」などといっている光景がテレビなどで報道されますが、これを見ている多く

"I'm so sorry to put you to this trouble."

"No, no. I'm sorry that I was of no help to you at all last time."

"What are you saying? I'm so grateful to you for what you've done."

"I'm afraid you're exaggerating. It's making me embarrassed."

This kind of conversation is repeated over and over without really going anywhere.

In the West, it's much simpler:

"Thank you very much for inviting me."

"Don't mention it. I appreciate your coming."

The greeting ends there. In Japan, the conversation won't progress without repeating this process two or three times.

Behind this custom lies the desire to be part of a group. Japanese value group harmony, and they don't like to stand out. In business situations, etiquette requires one first to listen to the opinion of the other person, then modestly add his or her own comment, just as one first pours beer for one's companion.

Also, if one doesn't accept another person's opinion, one does best by first looking to the boss, colleagues or subordinates within one's group, and ask, "Well, what do you think?" In this way the opinions of others can be determined before one proceeds indirectly or ambiguously to refute the speaker's comment.

There's a downside to this yielding, however. For example, often during some crisis or major world event, the Japanese government will be seen on TV saying, "We're observing the responses of other countries

の外国人は「なんて、頼りない、自主性のない国なんだ。こんな政府は信頼できないぞ」と思ってしまいます。譲り合いの精神は必ずしも日本国外では良いこととして受け入れられないのです。

first." When foreigners see this they may feel, "This country is unreliable. They lack the will or the capacity to make their own independent judgments. We can't trust their government." Mutual yielding is not necessarily viewed as a good thing outside Japan.

⑧ なぜ出る釘は打たれるの?

「出る釘は打たれる」という言葉があるように、日本ではあまり自分の意見を言いすぎたり、派手なことをしたりして、グループの中で突出する人は、排斥される傾向にあります。

ただ、この諺は、日本人の間ではどちらかというと、日本での賢い生き方を皮肉ったもので、日本人の多くは「出る釘は打たれる」という社会の弊害もちゃんと承知しているようです。

最近では、国家機構の構造疲労がよく議論の対象となり、「出る釘」こそはもっと延ばしてゆかなければという意見も聞かれるようになりました。とはいっても、例え「出る釘」をもっと認めようと思っている人でも、人前で相手の意見を攻撃したり、自らの能力を誇示したりする人を認めようとは思っていないのです。彼らのいう「出る釘」は、若くて優秀な人が、年功序列制度のためにその才能を発揮できないような社会、良いアイディアを持った人が、幾重にも積み重なった官僚機構の重圧につぶされていくような社会を改革するべきだという考え方です。

では、どういう人が日本では優秀な人とされるのでしょうか。また、どんな人が人格のあるリーダーとして認められるのでしょうか。ここで、「桃李ものいわざれども、下自ずから蹊をなす」という中国の諺を紹介しましょう。これは、優秀な人の所には、その人が別に何も話さなくても、自然に人が集まり道ができるものだということを意味しています。この諺に象徴されるように、優秀な人は自らの才能をPRしたりはせず、むしろ謙遜し、言葉も少なく落ちついているものだと考えられているのです。ですから、「私はこうだ、私はこれができる」と自分をPRする人が現

8 Why does the nail that sticks up get hammered down?

In Japan, those who stand out either by voicing their own opinions too directly or by exhibiting loud or showy behavior are typically rejected by the group. In other words, "The nail that sticks up gets hammered down."

While many Japanese understand the negative social climate created by this conformist way of thinking, they also cynically understand its importance for survival in Japanese society.

In recent years, for example, the outmoded government structure has become an object of frequent debate. Many people feel that "*deru kugi*" or "standing out" should be encouraged. But when people advocate "standing out," they are not voicing their support for those who attack others' opinions or aggressively show off their abilities. Rather, advocating "*deru kugi*" means reforming a society which prevents young, intelligent people from exercising their talent due to the seniority system, and where people with good ideas are crushed by bureaucratic pressure.

What type of person is valued and recognized as having leadership qualities in Japan? There is a Chinese proverb, "*Touri mono iwazaredomo, shita mizukara kei wo nasu.*" This can be translated as "People will naturally find their way to a wise man's door without him having to lead them there." It suggests that superior persons do not need to promote themselves. Instead, they are humble and low-key, and they choose their words carefully. Even advocates of "*deru kugi*" feel put off by someone who boasts, "I am such-and-such," or "I can do this or that."

れれば、「出る釘」を延ばしたいと思っている人でも、その人のことを不愉快に思ってしまうのです。

　加えて、人の立場を大切にする人を日本人は尊敬します。もし自分の意見を強調することで、その意見に反対している人の顔がつぶれるとわかったら、多くの日本人はできるだけその人との調整に努力してから、すべての人の立場に問題がないことを確認した上で、コメントを続けようとするのです。

　まず、自分の意見、自分の立場という意識が、日本では「出る釘」となり、利己的な行為として批判されるのです。黙って仕事を成し遂げる人。自分がものにした成功を強調せず、常に人から学ぼうという態度を忘れない人。そして、人と人との和を重んじながら、グループをまとめていける人。こうした人が、日本では優秀な人とみなされるのです。「出る釘」は、異なる文化背景の中では、その意味も違ってきます。英語でいう「アウトスタンディングである」とは、優秀で目立つ人を示しており、そうした人が自己の意見を強調したり、あるいは自己をPRすることは当然のことだと考えられています。ですから、アメリカ人からみると、日本人にとって優秀な人がそうでなく思えたりすることもあるのです。もちろん逆もまた真なりというところでしょう。

Furthermore, Japanese respect those who show sensitivity toward other people's positions. For example, if a Japanese notices that someone else is losing face when he or she is making a point, most would try to help that person save face by toning down any adverse comments, and continue their comments only after checking with the group to see whether or not there's a problem.

Consciously promoting your own opinion and position is regarded as self-centered and looked down upon in Japan. Instead, people who are seen as superior do their work silently, don't toot their own horn, try to learn from others, and can thus foster harmony among a group's members.

"Standing out" and "being outstanding" mean different things to different cultures. In the US, "outstanding" means that a person is superior and noteworthy. It is seen as natural for such people to express their own opinions and promote themselves. A person whom Japanese consider superior might not appear that way to Americans, and vice-versa.

9 なぜ日本人は遠慮するの？

　人前で自己を強く主張しない控えめな日本人。そんな日本人がよく使う言葉に「遠慮」があります。

　これはなかなか英語に翻訳しにくいのですが、あえていえば「躊躇する」とか「控えめに表現したり行動したりする」、「相手のじゃまをしないように気を使う」、さらにはそこから派生して「欠席する」とか「特定の行動をしないでおくこと」などが「遠慮」の意味する概念となります。

　日本人は人の家に招かれたとき、ホストから「お茶でもどうぞ」とすすめられると、「どうぞお構いなく」という風にそれにこたえます。

　これは日本人の遠慮という観念を最も端的に示した表現です。こう言うことによって客は、ホストがわざわざお茶を持ってくる手間に対して、気を使っているわけです。もちろん、客の方はお茶が嫌いなわけでも、ホストがお茶を出さないわけでもありません。これは人の家を訪問したときの儀式のようなもので、そういう控えめな応対をすることが、日本人の間で交流を進めてゆくための第一歩なのです。

　さて、それではアメリカではどうでしょうか。アメリカでも人の家に招かれると、やはりホストから「飲み物は何になさいますか」と聞かれるでしょう。すると、多くの人が、「どんなものがありますか？」と聞いたり、またはホストの家にありそうなものの中から好きなものを遠慮なく注文したりします。例えば「ソーダをいただけますか」とか「ビールはありますか」、あるいは「コーヒーをください」といったふうにリクエストをするはずです。

　従って、こうした風習の違いを知らずに、日本人がアメリカ人の家に招待されて、「お飲み物は」と尋ねられて、

Why do Japanese hold themselves back?

Most Japanese don't express their point of view strongly to other people. They refer to this as "*enryo*."

Although this word is difficult to translate into English, it roughly means "to hesitate," "to act or express oneself modestly," or "to be careful not to impose on others." Additional meanings include "to restrain oneself" and "to put off taking any specific action."

An example of this type of behavior is the following: When a Japanese is invited to someone's home, the host offers tea. The guest typically answers, "Please don't go to any trouble."

This expression best demonstrates the Japanese concept of "*enryo*." The guest's main concern is that the host doesn't go to the trouble of preparing and serving tea. However, saying this doesn't literally mean the guest doesn't want tea, or that the host won't in fact serve it. This formality is a type of ritual formula used when visiting someone's house. Not wanting to impose on others is the first step in interaction between Japanese.

What about in the US? When invited to someone's home you will probably be asked, "Can I get you something to drink?" Most Americans would either ask directly, "Sure, what do you have?" or go ahead and request something specific. For example, they might ask, "May I have a soda?" or "Do you have a beer?" or "Is there coffee?"

When Japanese unaware of this difference in custom are invited to an American's house, their behavior appears

「お構いなく」と言ったために、何か変な人と思われたケースも多いようです。

また、ひどいケースでは、アメリカ人の家にホームステイすることになった日本人の学生が、「どうぞ冷蔵庫から好きなものをとってね」と言われても、遠慮して、どうしても冷蔵庫が開けられずにお腹をすかしていたなんてこともありました。確かに、日本人からしてみれば、人の家の冷蔵庫を勝手に開けるなんて、ちょっと厚かましいような気がしますよね。そのホームステイ先の両親は共働きでいつも夕食の用意ができるわけではないので、冷蔵庫にはいつも十分な食べ物が入っていたのですが。その学生は、何度もお腹をすかせたままベッドに入りながら、ホームステイ先のホストを恨んだことでしょうが、実はホストの方も彼女の食欲がないことを心配していたわけです。

日本人は、他人同士、すなわち「外」の関係の人に向かっては特に「遠慮」して、自己を主張する行為を差し控えます。また、「親しき中にも礼儀あり」という言葉があるように、仲間内の関係になっても、相手が年上だったり、上司や先輩だったりすれば、当然遠慮しながら接してゆくことが常識ある態度ということになります。

問題はこの「遠慮」の概念が、外国人に大きな誤解を与えてしまうことです。自分の感情を正直に言わずに、遠慮して黙っていたり、100のところを20ぐらいしか言わなかったために、外国人がその「遠慮」した言葉や行為をそのままとってしまったり、この日本人はどうもはっきりとものの言えない能力のないやつだと思われてしまったりすることがあるのです。

日本では、相手が遠慮したとしても、それは単なるマナーだと知っておくことが大切です。その人が欲するであろうと思われるものを、礼儀正しくオファーして、その反応を見ることで、その人が本当に欲しいものを見つけることができるのです。時には何度かオファーを出してみなけれ

odd. Their response to the question "Can I get you something to drink?" is "Don't go to any trouble for me."

The situation can even become as extreme as the following incident. A Japanese student home-staying with an American family was told, "Please help yourself to anything in the refrigerator," but she held herself back even when she was in fact hungry. Japanese feel that helping yourself to what's in someone else's refrigerator is rather brazen. The parents in the home–stay family both worked and weren't always able to prepare dinner, though the refrigerator was always kept well stocked. The young student went to bed hungry several times and had bitter memories of her home–stay parents, who themselves were concerned about her apparent lack of appetite.

Japanese embrace "*enryo*" and refrain from putting themselves first, especially with outsiders. As the expression "Show your best manners even with people close to you" reveals, being reserved with others is common sense when the person is older, your boss, or your senior—even if he or she is part of your inner group.

Japanese don't express their true feelings entirely, but often put only 20% of what they want to say into words. Westerners end up thinking that Japanese are incapable of expressing themselves clearly. They tend to take Japanese reserve at face value. "*Enryo*" has thus been the cause of considerable misunderstanding for Westerners, who favor more open and outgoing behavior.

In Japan, when others are holding back, it is important to understand that their reserved behavior is simply good manners. You can find out what they want by politely offering what you think they might want, and then observing their response. It may take more than one

ば、相手の気持ちがつかめないかもしれませんが、そうしているうちに遠慮しているのか、本当に興味がないのかが分かってくるものです。

offer before they are willing to accept, but with practice you can learn the difference between a refusal out of modesty and one based on a genuine lack of interest.

10 なぜ日本人は歴史にこだわるの？

　時には過去と現在と未来がありますが、そのどこに重き
をおくかは、その国によって違いがあるようです。
　例えば、アメリカ人はどちらかというと、過去より現在
から未来を大切にします。それに対して、すでに触れまし
たように、日本人は過去から現在を見、その延長に未来を
見る傾向があります。例えば、日本人の場合、過去に何の
繋がりもない人や、どのような背景を持っているか分から
ない人とは、ビジネスを進めていくことを躊躇します。

　それに対してアメリカ人は、自分の要求を満たしてくれ
る人で、そこから未来が見渡せるなら誰とでも、比較的簡
単にビジネス上の関係を構築することができるのです。と
いうのも、アメリカ自体歴史の短い若い国ですから、過去
の背景にこだわっていては何も先には進められないからで
す。

　では、なぜ日本人は過去にそんなにこだわるのでしょう
か。それは、日本の歴史そのものと深い関係がありそうで
す。
　日本は島国ということもあって、ごく最近まで外国から
の脅威をそれほど受けずに独立を保ってきました。日本人
は長い年月に亘って、ずっと同じような身分制度を維持す
ることができたのです。一例を挙げれば、天皇制は、古代
に日本が国家として統一された頃から現在までずっと維持
されてきています。もちろん時代によって天皇の権限や権
威は様々に変化しましたが、これだけ長い間一つの王室が
存続した例は世界でもないのではないでしょうか。そして、
この天皇制の例と同じように、多くの身分制度が長い年月
の間、社会の中で温存されてきたのです。

10 Why are Japanese so concerned with background and the past?

Each country weighs the past, present and future differently.

For example, Americans value the present and the future over the past. But as we have seen, however, Japanese view the present in terms of the past, and the future is seen as an extension of past and present. Japanese are reluctant to establish business with someone who has no prior connection to them, or with someone whose background is unclear.

On the other hand, in America, if someone offers you something that meets your current needs, you can see the future potential. It is relatively easy to establish a business relationship. Compared to Japan, the United States is a young nation with a short history. It is thought that people can't move forward if they are too concerned with the past.

Why is Japan so fascinated with the past? The answer is related to Japanese history.

Japan is an island country. It did not have to consider the threat of invasion till very recently, and was able to maintain its independence. Social status systems were thus able to remain in place over a long period of time. The imperial system is one example. It has been preserved from the ancient past, when Japan was first unified as a nation, right up to the present. Naturally, over time the emperor's rights and authority changed drastically, but it is the oldest imperial system in the world. Other social status systems in Japanese society have also remained over time.

　従って、江戸時代以前はその人の背景、身分を知ることによって、その人にどのように接し、敬意を払えばよいか即座に判断できたのです。現在でこそ、身分制度はなくなりましたが、日本人の心の中には、相手の背景を知ることによって安心するという思考方法が残っていったのです。ですから、その個人が勤めている会社、卒業した大学などが、その個人を評価する一つの基準になっています。

　また、会社を評価するときでさえも、現在の実績よりも、過去にどのようなことをしてきたかといったことで、多くの人が評価するようです。

　今後、経済が世界とつながってゆく中で、日本人はよりいっそう海外と交流してゆかなければならなくなります。そうしたとき、得てして差別ともとられかねないようなこうした古い慣習を改め、膚の色、国籍、家庭の事情などといった、その人の背景でものごとを判断したりせずに、すべての人や人種を平等に取り扱うようにしてゆくことは、もっとも大切なことの一つではないかと思うのです。

Before the end of Edo period, an awareness of someone's background or social status helped determine how they should be treated and the measure of respect they should be given. Even though such strict status systems are no longer in place today, Japanese still feel more secure knowing a person's background. Standards by which individuals are judged include their company, university and so on.

Furthermore, many people judge a company more by its past performance than by its current results.

As more and more Japanese interact with the world because of an increasingly globalized business environment, it is of utmost importance that they improve such behavior, which may be considered discriminatory, and treat every individual, of any race, equally, as opposed to judging them based upon their background, including skin color, nationality, or family history.

11 なぜ日本人はあんなにプライドが高いの?

　多少でも日本人と付き合ったことのある外国人なら、日本人の控えめな態度の中に、実に強いプライドが隠されているような気がしてくるはずです。

　日本人は世界の中でも、海外で自分たちがどのように評価されているかを特に気にする国民のようです。実際、海外での日本評についての記事や報道の多さにはただただ驚くばかりです。それこそが、逆の意味で日本人のプライドを示す好材料なのかもしれません。

　日本は17世紀以降、200年以上国を閉ざし、海外との交流を絶っていました。そして、1853年にペリー提督がやってきたとき、その200年の間に、世界が大きく変化し、日本が近代化した他の国に比べて大きく立ち遅れてしまったことに気づいたのです。

　それから間もなく、1867年に近代国家として生まれ変わって以来、日本は国をあげて世界のレベルに追いつけ追い越せと、懸命に努力をしてきました。そして、努力の甲斐あって、ほんの数十年のうちに日本は当時の列強の仲間入りをすることができたのです。

　こうした努力の過程で、日本人の心の中には、海外と比べて日本がどうなのかということへの異様な好奇心が育成されていったようです。そして、そんな好奇心と共に、外国から侮られないように自分の国を良く見せたいという意識がどんどん強くなっていったのでしょう。

　この意識こそが、外国人の見る日本人のプライドなのではないでしょうか。19世紀の後半に、当時の井上馨という外務大臣は、鹿鳴館という西洋風の迎賓館をつくって、そこで各国の外交官を招きパーティーを何度も開きました。そして、「どうです、日本も西洋と変わらないでしょう」と

11 Why are Japanese so proud?

Foreigners who spend some time with Japanese probably notice a great deal of pride hidden beneath their modest exteriors.

Japanese are particularly concerned with what people of other nations think of them. The degree to which the Japanese media focuses on foreign criticism and perceptions of Japan is truly amazing. Ironically, this preoccupation also reveals the pride of Japanese.

Historically, Japan closed its borders in the seventeenth century and was isolated for two hundred years. When Admiral Perry came to Japan in 1853, Japanese realized how much the world had changed over the course of those years and how far behind they had fallen.

In 1868, Japan opened its doors to the West and was reborn as a modern country. The entire nation devoted itself to catching up with international standards, and to surpassing them. As a result of those efforts, Japan joined the ranks of the powerful nations of the world within a few decades.

Japanese developed an unusual curiosity about how they fared compared to foreigners. They also wanted to make their country look good to the world so that foreigners could not make fools of them.

These trends are probably a reflection of Japanese pride. In the latter half of the nineteenth century, Foreign Minister Inoue Kaoru built Rokumeikan, a Tokyo guest house for dignitaries. He often invited foreign diplomats there for parties and reportedly boasted,

自慢したといわれています。また、そうした井上の行為は「西洋崇拝」であり、日本を侮辱するものだという人たちが、彼を暗殺しようとした事件も起きています。

　井上馨も、彼を暗殺しようとした人も、どちらもコインの裏と表のように、日本人のプライドのあり方を代弁しています。

　戦後、日本は再び戦争の傷のために海外から大きく水をあけられました。そして、あの1867年以降と同じように頑張って、またも世界に大きな影響を与える国へと成長したのです。

　そして、今もなお、日本人の心の中には、やはり井上馨と彼の暗殺をたくらんだ人物の二つの心が同居しているように思えます。

　1980年代、日本が経済的に成長を遂げ、世界の注目を集めたとき、井上馨の亡霊は、「そうです。もう日本は世界の中でもトップクラスの国どころか、海外から学ぶものがないほどにまで成長したのです」と言ったことでしょう。

　それに対して、井上に反対する亡霊たちは、「この大成功こそは、日本人が昔から勤勉で、礼儀正しく、日本独自の文化が育んできた価値観を守ってきたからこそ成し遂げられたんだ。日本人は海外の人たちよりも豊かな文化を持った優秀な民族なんだ」と言ったことでしょう。

　どうですか、心当たりはありませんか。

　ただ、日本人とより深く交流したいと思うなら、外国人も日本人のこの複雑な心理構造を理解することをお勧めします。そうすれば、商談やビジネスでの接待などのときでも、注意して話題を選ぶことができるようになるはずです。

郵 便 は が き

１１２

料金受取人払

小石川局承認

1247

差出有効期間
平成11年6月
19日まで

（誤解される日本人）

愛読者カード係

インターナショナル　行

講談社

東京都文京区音羽一丁目

十七番十四号

★この本についてお気づきの点，ご感想などをお教えください。

　　今後の出版企画の参考にいたしたく存じます。ご記入のうえご投函くださいますようお願いいたします（平成11年6月19日までは切手不要です）。

a　ご住所　　　　　　　　　　　　　　　　　〒□□□-□□

b　お名前　　　　　　　　　　　　c　年齢（　　　）歳

　　　　　　　　　　　　　　　　　d　性別　1男性　2女性

e　ご職業　　1大学生　2短大生　3高校生　4中学生　5各種学校生徒
　　　　　　6教職員　7公務員　8会社員(事務系)　9会社員(技術系)　10会社役員
　　　　　　11研究職　12自由業　13サービス業　14商工従事　15自営業　16農林漁業
　　　　　　17主婦　18家事手伝い　19無職　20その他（　　　　　　　　　　　）

f　本書をどこでお知りになりましたか。
　　　1新聞広告(新聞名　　　　　　)　2雑誌広告(雑誌名　　　　　　)
　　　3書評(書名　　　　　　　)　4実物を見て　5人にすすめられて
　　　6その他(　　　　　　　　　)

g　どんな本を対訳で読みたいか、お教えください。

h　どんな分野の英語学習書を読みたいか、お教えください。

御協力ありがとうございました。

"You see, Japan is not so different from the West after all." However, certain Japanese thought Inoue was humiliating Japan in mimicking Western styles and customs, and they attempted to assassinate him.

Inoue Kaoru and the people who attempted to assassinate him were exhibiting the two extremes of Japanese pride.

After World War II, Japan had to rebuild itself again, just as it had done in 1868. It made a concerted effort to catch up, and became one of the most influential countries in the world.

But many Japanese are still of two minds—that of Inoue Kaoru, and that of his assassins.

In the 1980's, Japan received worldwide attention for its economic success. At that time, the ghost of Inoue Kaoru might have said, "Well, Japan is now as good or better than the Western industrial nations." The ghosts of his would-be assassins would have responded, "This great success is a result of the fact that historically Japanese were diligent, had proper manners, and preserved the values of Japan's unique culture. Japanese culture is richer than foreign cultures, and the Japanese are a superior people."

Does this sound familiar?

If you want to have a close relationship with Japanese, it is wise to be aware of this complex Japanese psychology and adapt your topics of conversation when doing business.

12 なぜ日本人は日本は安全で清潔な国だというの？

　日本は安全で清潔な国だと思っている日本人は、相当な数にのぼるのではないでしょうか。

　アトランタ・オリンピックのとき、公園が何者かによって爆破され、死傷者がでた事件がありました。そのすぐ後アメリカ人のジャーナリストが、次の冬季オリンピックの開催地である長野に行って、日本での安全対策について一般の人の意見を聞きました。すると、ほとんどの人が、「日本ではあんなことはおきないと思いますよ」と答えたのです。

　世界がますます狭く、そしてダイナミックに交流している現在では、どこか特定の国だけが安全だということは、もはやなくなってしまいました。現在は、我々一人一人の安全を世界中が協力して考えてゆかなければならない時代なのです。すなわち、日本だけは別という考え方自体がすでに通用しなくなってきているのです。

　日本が安全だという神話の背景には、日本の警察は優秀だからというもう一つの神話があります。また、日本は少数の民族によって構成されているから外国よりは統率がとれやすいという思いも日本人の間にはあるのでしょう。

　しかし、グローバルな時代ともいえる現在では、こうした発想自体が過去のものになりつつあることを、日本人も知っておく必要があるのではないでしょうか。

　安全の神話が特に強く語られるようになったのは、80年代に入ってからではないかと思います。日本経済の力が急速に成長し、世界に大きな影響を与えるようになった80年代に、多くの日本人が自らの成功を誇り、その理由をあれこれと説明しました。また、それとは対照的に様々な社会問題に悩んでいたアメリカは、日本の繁栄に驚き、日本の

12 Why do Japanese say that Japan is a safe and clean country?

A great many Japanese feel that Japan is a safe and clean country. Just after the fatal bombing at Olympic Park during the Atlanta Olympics, an American journalist went to Nagano, the site of the 1998 winter Olympics. He asked people their opinions about Japanese security policies. Practically every one asked responded, "That sort of thing would never happen in Japan."

The world is becoming smaller and more dynamic. These days, it is no longer possible to say that one particular country is safer than another. This is an age where we have to work together globally to insure individual safety. We should get beyond assuming that Japan is protected and special.

Behind Japan's myth of safety is another myth: that this safety is due to Japan's superior police force. As explained earlier, the notion also exists that since Japanese are a homogeneous people, leadership is easier there than in foreign countries.

Japanese need to know that this way of thinking is fast becoming obsolete.

This myth about safety has been around since the 1980's, when Japan's economic power was growing rapidly and greatly influencing the world. Many Japanese were proud of their success and offered a variety of reasons for it. Conversely, America was plagued by a myriad of social problems and was surprised by

成功に興味を示し、マスコミも様々なテーマで日本の成功の秘密を取り上げました。

こうした中で、安全な日本というイメージができあがっていったのでしょう。そして、日本人が、そうしたイメージを喜び自慢したこともまた事実だったようです。確かに80年代に日本人が抱いた成功の喜びと、自惚れともいえる優越感は、バブルがはじけ、日本経済、そして日本の社会自体が大きく変化しようとしている現在でもまだ、日本人の心の中に深い影響を与えているようです。

ところで、安全と同じく、日本人が常に心に抱いているプライドの一つに、日本人は清潔だからという神話があります。薬害エイズの問題や、堺市の食中毒の問題など、日本人の健康を脅かす様々な問題が、そうした清潔神話を崩そうとしています。

元々エイズは海外から日本に上陸した病気です。また、堺市の食中毒についても、同様のケースが数年前にすでにアメリカで報告されていました。そう、清潔の問題も、安全と同様に、一つの国だけで片づけられる問題ではなくなっているのです。「日本は安全です」とか「日本は清潔です」とかいうコメントは、ただ日本を世界から孤立させるだけで、そこから何もよいことは生まれてきません。

多くの外国人は、それを聞くと、日本人は自分たちは自然に対して免疫があり、他の人たちには起こる人災も自分たちだけは免れることができるのか、と思ってしまいます。しかし多くの日本人が、松本や東京の地下鉄でおきたサリン事件、それに神戸の大震災をきっかけに、今までの安全への考え方を変えようとしているのです。

控えめなプライドの殻に閉じこもるのではなく、世界と協力し、交流して安全や健康の問題に取り組む姿勢が日本人にも欲しいものです。

Japan's prosperity. It took a great interest in Japan's success, and the American media reported on the secrets of this success from many angles.

The image of Japan as a safe country emerged under the glare of all this attention. Actually, the Japanese were pleased with their successes and boasted about them. However, this sense of superiority continued to have a deep impact on Japanese thinking even after the so-called "bubble" burst and the Japanese economy and society began to experience major upheavals.

Another source of Japanese pride is the myth of extraordinary cleanliness. Various public health disasters, such as the AIDS infection spread to haemophiliacs through tainted blood supply, and the food poisoning in the town of Sakai, have dispelled this myth.

AIDS was originally brought to Japan from abroad, and cases of food poisoning similar to that of Sakai were reported several years prior in America. It is clear that neither public health issues nor safety issues can be solved by one country alone. But comments like "Japan is totally safe" and "Japan is totally clean" only serve to isolate Japan further. Nothing good comes from them.

When foreigners hear comments like this, they are mostly amazed that Japanese consider themselves immune to natural or manmade disasters that plague the rest of humanity. Many Japanese have started to reevaluate their previous sense of security in the light of incidents such as the gas attacks in the town of Matsumoto and the Tokyo subway, or the devastating earthquake in Kobe.

I hope that Japanese will stop withdrawing into their shell of pride and work more closely with the rest of the world to address common safety and public health issues.

13 なぜ日本人は自分たちを「ユニーク」だと思っているの？

　日本はますます世界の他の国々と強い結び付きを持つようになり、他の先進国が抱えるのと同様の問題に悩まされるようになっているというのに、それでもまだ日本人は、自分たちのことを「ユニーク」だと言います。なぜでしょうか。

　多くの日本人は理路整然と順序立ててものごとを説明しなくても、相手に自分の意思を以心伝心で伝えることができると思っているものですから、いきなり外国人から10言いたいことがあるならば、その10すべてにわたって、きちんと分かりやすく説明して欲しいと言われても、戸惑うばかりで、なかなか良い方法が見つかりません。そうした時に、日本人は苦肉の策で「いやね。日本は違うんですよ」とやってしまうのです。しかし、外国人からみれば、これでは何の答えにもなりません。いったい日本はどのように違うのかということを、感情からではなく冷静に話してもらいたいと思うのです。

　これが英語での会話となると、日本人はハンディがあるものですからうまく相手に説得できず、「というのも、日本には外国にないユニークな文化があるんです」と答えてしまうのですが、これでますます外国人は混乱してしまうのです。

　「ユニークな文化」と言うのではなく、例えば「日本では例え理由はなくても相手の会社に顔を出し、少しずつ人間関係をつくってゆくやり方があって、そのようなプロセスを踏まえてはじめてビジネスが大きく前進するんです……」といったような明快な説明をすればいいのです。

　ところが、理論的にどんどん追いつめられ、何か提案すると「なぜ」といって切りかえされてばかりいると、「ああ、この人にはどうせ分かりはしないや」という捨て鉢な気分

13 Why do Japanese still say they are unique?

If Japan has become integrated with the rest of the world and suffers from many of the same problems as other advanced nations, why do some Japanese still insist on claiming that they are unique?

Many Japanese believe that they can convey their thoughts to each other via "*ishin-denshin*," or non-verbal communication, and don't need to explain things logically and systematically. They run into problems when foreigners tell them that if they want to say ten things, they should explain all ten. This is when Japanese start saying " Japan is different" as a last resort. The Westerner feels he or she can't get a straight answer, and wishes the Japanese would explain calmly and logically exactly how Japanese practices are different in a particular situation.

If the conversation is in English, this is a handicap for the Japanese. When pressed, it becomes more difficult to respond, so he or she replies, "What I mean is that Japan has a unique culture." This only further confuses the foreigner.

It would be better for the Japanese to give a concrete example: "In Japan, for instance, we show up at our customer's company for no particular reason. By doing this, relationships are gradually strengthened and business can take great initial leaps."

However, if the Westerner continues to dispute his logic and keeps rebutting him, the Japanese may give up, thinking, "Oh, this guy just doesn't understand."

にもなって、ついつい、外国人にとっては何の意味もない、ナショナリズムともとられかねない発言をしてしまうのでしょう。

従って、海外から来た人が、このような言葉を日本人から聞くと、むっとして、日本人は心が狭く、プライドばかり高いと誤解してしまったとしても、仕方ないかもしれません。

日本人側は、外国人との交流では日本の常識でコミュニケーションしてもだめなんだということをもう一度考えて、相手をどのように説得するかという方法について、じっくりと対策を練り直してゆくことが大切です。

語彙や英語力そのものに問題がある場合は、できるだけ説得力のある具体例を多く用意しておくことも一案ですし、表情やジェスチャーを豊かに使いこなし、にこやかなムードで会話を続けるこつを学ぶことも大切です。

こうしたことを踏まえながら、たどたどしい英語でも、具体的で明快なメッセージを伝えるようにすれば、相手と積極的に交流できるのだということを知っておく必要があるのです。

双方が歩み寄り、相手に対して思いやりをもつことが、生産的でないナショナリズムの対立を未然に防ぐことができる、ただ一つの方法なのではと思うのですがいかがでしょうか。

Then there's a risk that the Westerner will misconstrue this attitude as crude nationalism.

Consequently, it stands to reason that foreigners get offended and misconstrue the Japanese as narrow-minded and proud.

Once again, it is important that Japanese don't communicate with foreigners only according to Japanese ideas of common sense. Rather, they should try to adapt their methods in order to get foreigners to understand.

When vocabulary or language ability is a problem, it helps to use concrete examples wherever possible. Concrete examples have persuasive power. It is also important to learn how to move a conversation along through an awareness of the expressivity of facial expressions and gestures, and a positive attitude.

It is much better for Japanese to try to convey a concrete and clear message, even in imperfect English, than to wrap things up with a patronizing smile and the words, "That being said, Japan is a unique homogeneous nation." This is an important thing to remember when doing business with Westerners.

In truth, there's only one way to prevent statements that smack of chauvenism and lead to unproductive confrontations: each side must try putting themselves in the other's shoes.

第3章
日本の職場のミステリー

●

CHAPTER 3

Mysteries of
the Japanese Workplace

なぜ日本人は仕事が終わっても帰らないの?

　なぜ就業時間が終わっても日本人は働いているのだろうと、欧米の人たちは、不思議に思っていることでしょう。日本では午後5時というのは、単に会社で定められた就業時間が終了したというだけで、それ以降はプライベートな時間であるという意味ではありません。むしろ、何か特別なことでもないかぎり、午後5時きっかりに職場を離れる人はそういないのです。

　なぜ、日本人はそんなに遅くまで働くのでしょうか。遅くまで働くことによって、欧米の人たちよりも多くの物を生産したり、考え出したりしているのでしょうか。

　欧米の人にとっては、こうした日本人の行為は不可解でなりません。もちろん彼らの中にも、家族との夕食を犠牲にしてまで、会社に忠誠を誓う人もいるでしょうが。

　他のアジア諸国でも見られる傾向ですが、日本では、仕事をするためには、まずお互いに知り合いになって、十分に人間関係を構築しなければなりません。ビジネス上の条件がいかに折り合っても、お互いが知らない者同士であった場合、日本人はなかなか一緒に仕事をしないのです。

　従って、日本の会社では、人間関係を構築するために、取引先や新規の顧客を頻繁に訪ねてゆきます。管理職や営業関係の人は、そうした訪問やミーティングに一日のほとんどを割いているのです。そして、夕方になってはじめて、問い合わせのあった商品の調査をしたり、伝票を整理したりといったデスクワークにかかるのです。また、日本では欧米に比べ一つのことを決裁するのに、できるだけ多くの人のコンセンサスをとろうとします。従って、その分だけ打ち合わせや承認を得るためだけの会議が頻繁に開かれます。これも、会社員が日中に実務をこなす時間を縮める原因です。

Why don't Japanese go home right after work?

Westerners often wonder why Japanese continue to work after hours. In Japan, however, 5 o'clock just means the end of the official work-day. "Unofficial" work usually continues into the night—unless there are extenuating circumstances. Rarely does "after five" mean private time.

Why do Japanese work so late? Are Japanese more productive than Westerners because of their late hours?

This kind of behavior is hard for Westerners to understand, though some Westerners feel great loyalty to their companies, giving up dinner with their families in order to get the job done.

In Japan, as in other Asian countries, people have to get to know each other and build a good relationship before they start to do business. Even though you may agree about work-related affairs, you can't really be part of the team if you're a stranger.

People in Japanese companies frequently visit the offices of their important clients and new customers. Practically the entire day of a manager or salesperson consists of such visits and meetings. Thus, they don't really begin to tackle the accumulated desk-work—such as invoicing and product research—until evening. Also, Japanese try to achieve consensus among as many people as possible before making a decision. This requires frequent discussion meetings just to gain approval, and eats into available work time during the day.

こうした理由で、多くの人は午後5時頃になってはじめて自分の机に戻り、落ちついてたまった仕事をかたづけるのです。

そして、夕方になれば、顧客を訪問していた社員も、会議に出席していた部長も、さらには研修に行っていた若手社員も、みんなオフィスに戻ってきます。ちょうど家族がみんなそろったように、それぞれの部署で部員が顔を合わせられるのが、この午後5時以降なのです。

最近でこそ増えてはきましたが、それでも日本では、欧米に比べて転職率が少ないこともあって、長い年月に亘って同じ顔ぶれで仕事をすることになります。従って、彼らは単にビジネスを通したドライな間柄ではなく、もっとプライベートな部分まで踏み込んだ、親密な関係を作っています。

そうした部員が午後5時を過ぎると部署に集まり、リラックスしながらその日にあったこと、顧客に関するゴシップ、あるいは社内での出来事などを話し、情報を交換したりするのです。

こうした交流の輪の中に入り、ネットワーキングを行う意味も含めて、日本人は5時以降もオフィスに残るのです。そして、午後7時頃になると、上司と部下とが連れだって、お酒を飲みにくり出すこともあります。そう、彼らはいつでも遅くまで働いているのではなく、遅くまでオフィスに残ることによって、人間関係を構築しているのです。ですから、プロダクティビティの面からみるならば、それほど生産的とはいえないのです。

This is why most people return to the office for the first time at about five o'clock, where they relax and deal with the work piled up on their desk.

When evening falls, many people return to the office, including employees who were out visiting customers, department managers who were in meetings, and rookie employees who were in training all day. This is when staff members of the various departments get to see each other, just like a family.

In Japan, employee turnover is low, especially when compared to the West, although it has increased somewhat in recent years. The same staff members have worked together for a long time. Theirs are not just "dry" relationships derived from business, but close relationships which extend to the personal.

Department members get together after five to relax and discuss what happened during the day, exchanging customer-related gossip or information about internal affairs.

Japanese stay late in order to be part of the circle of communication and to network. At about seven, bosses and their underlings sometimes go out drinking together. It's not that Japanese always stay late to work. Rather, they stay late to build relationships. In real terms, the practice is not all that productive.

2 なぜ日本人は場所を変えると態度が変わるの?

　日本人とお酒を呑みにいった外国人がびっくりすることの一つに、あんなに固い姿勢をして、かしこまっていた日本人が、お酒の席では人が変わったようにオープンになるのは、なぜなのだろういうことがあります。

　日本人が、お酒の席ではよく本音を語るということは前にも説明しましたが、ここで日本人にとって、特に日本でビジネスをする上で大切な、「場」という概念について説明しておきましょう。

　アメリカには「ワン・ミニット・マネージャー」という言葉があります。これは、マネージャーとして部下に注意をしたり、賞賛を与えたり、または指示を出す場合には、その場で、その時に伝えることが良しとされるということです。一分間というような短い時間、つまり物事がおきたその時点で、的確で簡潔な指示を出せる人を能力のあるマネージャーだとアメリカ人は思うのです。

　しかし、日本ではこうした概念は必ずしも当てはまりません。日本では、公式と非公式との「場」をうまく使い分けるからです。公式とはオフィスの中であり、あるいは会議の場であったりします。非公式とは、個人と個人とが別の場所で出会って、意見を交換し、それを調整することを意味します。お酒の付き合いはもちろんこの非公式の場にあたります。

　もし、あなたが会議の席で出された提案に反対だったとします。しかし、そこで公に反対の意見を言えば、それを提案した人の顔をつぶしてしまうかもしれません。特に相手が自分より立場が上であったり、大切な顧客であったりした場合はなおさらです。

　従って、あなたはその会議の「場」ではあまり強く反対意

2 Why do Japanese act differently in different environments?

Foreigners who go out drinking with Japanese are often surprised when someone rigid and polite suddenly opens up after a few drinks. It's almost as if he or she has become a different person entirely.

It was mentioned previously that Japanese express their opinions more directly when out drinking. The reason has to do with the concept of "*ba*" (place/occasion), which is very important in doing business in Japan.

America has the phrase "One-minute Manager." This refers to the idea that it is good for a manager to warn, praise, or give instructions to staff members at that very moment. Americans feel that someone who can give easy-to-follow instructions quickly and succinctly is a capable manager.

The "One-minute Manager" might not function so effectively in Japan, however, where people carefully differentiate between formal and informal places or environments. "Official" or formal places are the office, meeting rooms, or conferences. "Unofficial" or informal places are neutral locations where one meets to exchange and elaborate on individual opinions. Of course, bars are informal, "unofficial" places.

Let's assume that during a meeting, you disagree with someone else's idea. If you disagree in public, it may cause the other person to lose face, especially if that person is your superior or an important client.

Therefore, during the meeting, you shouldn't dis-

見を述べたりしません。しかし、あなたは自分の意見をぜ
ひ通したいと思った場合には次のような方法をとります。
まずは、第三者に調整を依頼します。そのとき、あなたは
つかつかとその調停者の机に行って自らの意見を述べる代
わりに、夕食などを利用した、リラックスした雰囲気で意
見を交換します。正しい「場」を設定することは、日本でビ
ジネスを行う上で極めて大切なことなのです。

　こうした「場」では、通常は距離のある上司との関係が大
幅に縮まります。従って、部下も会社が抱えている課題な
どについて、上司に率直な意見を述べたりします。

　そして、ビジネス上の重要なメッセージがこの酒宴の後
で伝えられることもよくあります。例えば、リラックスし
て心を開きあった後の帰りのタクシーで、次の商談の約束
を口頭で取り付けたり、決裁権を持った人物が、どのよう
に思っているかといった会話がなされることもあるので
す。

　そしてその翌日になると、また公式な「場」に誰もが戻り、
昨夜の騒ぎなどなかったかのように振る舞うのです。とこ
ろが、不思議なことに昨日までの問題が解決していたり、
それまでスムーズにいっていなかったビジネス上の課題が
さっと片づいたりするのです。

　非公式な「場」の力はすごいものです。しかも、誰も昨日
の酒の席での、あるいは帰りのタクシーの中での口約束の
ことなど触れもしません。また、同じように会議が始まり、
多くの人はかしこまって、ただ黙ってそれに参加していま
す。

　「私の仕事？　それはね、お客さんにお酒を呑ませること
さ」。ある日本人の部長はそのように言っていました。彼
は冗談を言っているのではありません。こうした非公式な
ネットワークをいかに巧みに使い分け、人間関係を構築し
てゆくかが、日本でビジネスを成功させる秘訣なのです。

　これこそは、「ワン・ミニット・マネージャー」を良しと

agree with the other person's opinion. However, if you insist on expressing your opposition, you might do it in the following way: ask for mediation. Then, exchange ideas in a casual location with the third party present. Don't do this in the office. In Japan, it's extremely important to create the right occasion for such situations.

The distance between boss and subordinate also lessens. Therefore, the subordinate can express his or her honest opinion about company issues and problems.

Important messages about business are often conveyed following a drinking session. For instance, it is not uncommon for people to make the next deal in the taxi ride home, since they feel relaxed and open, or they may talk about the decision maker's opinion in a casual manner.

The next day everyone returns to the original "*ba*"(location) and acts as if nothing happened the night before—with one exception. Mysteriously, yesterday's problems are now solved, or business affairs which had been stalled are now settled.

Unofficial or informal "*ba*" provide a powerful tool. No one mentions the verbal promises which were made while drinking or while in the taxi going home the night before. Meetings begin as usual and people sit quietly and politely during them.

A Japanese department manager once said, "My job is to let my client drink." He wasn't joking. How well you use the informal network and build interpersonal relationships is key in making business succeed in Japan.

Foreigners who admire the "One-minute Manager"

する外国人にとって、最も分かりづらい、そして永遠に解
明できない日本のミステリーなのです。

might find the concept of "*ba*" hard to understand. For them, it's a Japanese mystery that will remain unsolved.

③ なぜ日本人は物事を決めるのに あんなに時間がかかるの？

　欧米の人が日本人と仕事をしていて最も苛立つのは、物事をなかなか決裁してくれないことではないでしょうか。

　担当者でありながら、その人はイエスともノーとも言ってくれません。しかも、いろいろと資料や情報は要求するのですが、その後それがどのように使用されたかまったく知らされず、ただじっと待たされるものですから、人によっては、担当者はいったい何をしているんだろう、本当に能力があるんだろうか、と疑問をもったりすることもあるでしょう。

　日本では、担当者に与えられる決裁権が外国に比べて狭いのです。理由は簡単で、日本の場合、物事を決めるには、社内のコンセンサスを必要とするからです。すなわち、一つのプロジェクトを進める場合、そこに直接かかわる人物だけではなく、そのプロジェクトを完成に導くために必要なあらゆる部門、そして管理する立場の人の承認まで得なければ進行できないのです。

　下は一担当者から上は社長までが了承し、あらゆるリスクをつぶし、必要ならばたたき台を改善して、はじめて公に決裁しプロジェクトが動き出します。

　ですから、一度プロジェクトが動き出すと、今度はそれを変更したり中止したりすることが困難になります。日本では決裁に相当時間のかかった分だけ、短期間に総力を挙げてプロジェクトを完成させるのです。

　それに対して、欧米では、予算が許せば、担当者、あるいはその部内のレベルで比較的簡単にプロジェクトを動かすことができます。そのため、この感覚で日本の決裁の過程をみていると、いったいいつになったら物事が動き出す

3 **Why do Japanese take so long to make decisions?**

One thing that irritates Westerners extremely is Japanese businesspeople's refusal to make fast decisions.

Even when the person is in charge, he or she won't give a definite "yes" or "no." Instead, you'll probably be asked for lots of resources and information, but you won't know how they're going to be used and will be forced to wait it out. You might even begin to question your contact person's competence.

In Japan, an individual's decision-making authority is more limited than in other countries. The reason is simple: in Japan, internal company consensus is required in order to make a major decision. A project can't progress without the approval—not only of those directly involved, but also of various departments that will help bring the project to completion, and those in management as well.

A project is publicly begun only after approval all the way up to the company president has been received. All the many risks must be foreseen and the necessary revisions carried out in order for it to gain full approval.

Therefore, once a project is begun it is hard to change or abandon it. A project is usually completed in a short amount of time, since it has already taken so much time to make the decision and everyone is behind it.

In the West, a project can be initiated relatively easily by the contact person, or at the departmental level if the budget permits. When Westerners come across the Japanese decision-making process for the first time,

のか分からずに、困惑してしまうのです。

　ただ、アメリカなどの決裁の方法では、一度決裁したからと言って、リスクをすべてつぶし、あらゆる人の了承を得たわけではないので、計画が途中で現実にあわせた形で変更になることも得てしてあります。また、その時の経済事情でスケジュールが遅れたり、予算が変更になったりということも間々あります。すなわち、欧米の方法では、決裁の後に試行錯誤がはじまるのです。

　この決裁に関する考え方の違いを知らないために、大きな誤解が生まれることがあります。例えば、アメリカ人は、決裁をした後でも予定を変更しようとしますが、日本側はなかなかそれができません。

　従って、アメリカ人は日本人を柔軟性のない人々だと思います。また、決裁のあとに予定を変更するアメリカ人を日本側からみれば、時間にルーズで責任感がない人々だと誤解するわけで、実際にアメリカで働く日本人の多くがアメリカ人が締め切りを守らないことに不満をおぼえています。

　もちろん、双方の決裁方法には、長所もあれば短所もあります。日本のやり方では、じっくりと土台を固めて決裁を行いますから、実行にうつす時には、隙間なく緻密なプロジェクトのアウトラインができているわけです。が、反面、そこに至るまで時間がかかっているため、緊急な場合や、状況の急激な変化に対しては脆さを露呈します。

　アメリカ流のやり方は、迅速かつ行動的で、激しい競争に打ち勝つためには有効でしょう。しかし、途中で決裁の内容がどんどん変化してゆくため、海外との共同事業では摩擦が起こりやすく、また従業員や下請け業者からみれば、

they are often confused since they don't know when things really "start."

In the U.S. and other places, a project or plan can be changed along the way, since all the risks were not necessarily accounted for when the initial decision was made. Additionally, the schedule is often delayed due to economic factors, and the budget revised. After the decision is made, a process of trial and error begins to bring the process to fruition.

Great misunderstandings arise when people are unaware of these differences in decision making. Americans can readily change plans after a decision is made, but this is most often almost impossible in Japan.

Americans therefore, get the idea that Japanese are inflexible. And Japanese misunderstand Americans who propose changes late in the decision-making process—they feel they're wasting time and lack a sense of responsibility. Actually, many Japanese who work in the United States feel frustrated that Americans don't keep deadlines.

Certainly both decision-making methods have their strengths and weaknesses. The Japanese strength is that they take time to lay a solid foundation before the initial decision, so they have a very detailed project outline with few glitches in its execution. On the other hand, they're vulnerable to rapid changes in circumstances or urgent situations, and since it's taken so much time to arrive at the initial decision, they don't have a lot of leeway in the remaining schedule.

The American decision-making style is useful for winning tough competition, because it is quick and action-oriented. However, friction with overseas partners occurs easily since the initial agreement is likely to

最後まで会社を信頼して計画に没頭することにリスクを感じることもあるでしょう。

　日本の場合、決裁するまでにあるゆる人の理解を得ようとするために、その途上で必要な資料や統計、過去の事例などを収集し、上層部の納得を得るようにしなければなりません。そして少しでもリスクがあれば、もう一度話し合い、それを回避する方策を考えます。こうした過程の度に、企画書を提出したアメリカ人に問い合わせがいくものですから、日本流の決裁方法を知らないアメリカ人は、「いったい日本人は何をやっているんだ。こんなに我々に協力を求めていながら、何も起こらないなんて、本当に信用できるんだろうか」と考えてしまいます。お互いにその時々の状況を分かりやすく説明し、柔軟性を持って対応しないと、こうした誤解がとんでもない不幸な結末へと発展した例は枚挙にいとまがありません。

keep changing. Employees and subcontractors may start to feel it is risky to trust the company and think twice about putting all their effort into the plan.

Consensus is necessary in making the initial decision, so Japanese must gather the necessary resources, statistics and past precedents along the way in order to persuade top management. If there's even the slightest risk, they discuss it again and formulate an avoidance plan. Each time this occurs, the Japanese ask more questions of the Americans who submitted the plan. Americans who don't understand the Japanese decision-making style think, "What are those Japanese doing?! They demanded cooperation from us, but nothing's happening. I wonder if I can trust them." If circumstances aren't explained in an understandable way, and if responses to such an explanation aren't flexible, this kind of misunderstanding can have unfortunate results.

4 なぜ日本人は一度決めたら変えないの？

　欧米人の多くは、決裁までの長いプロセスは分かった、だがそれにしても日本人は、一度決めたことにこだわりすぎる、と思っているかもしれません。「もう少し柔軟に対応してくれないだろうか。もう何年も前に決めたことにこだわって、現実を見極めないのはおかしいんじゃないか」

　確かに日本人は一度決めたことを、なかなか変更しようとはしません。なぜでしょうか。

　その理由は、根回しというプロセスに関係しています。根回しとは、もともと植物を移植するときの言葉で、根元の周囲を掘り起こして、主な根を残して他の根を切っておき、鬚根を発生させて移植を容易にすることです。しかし、現在では根回しは、日本のビジネスカルチャーを代表する言葉となってしまいました。

　ビジネス上での根回しとは、公式の場で提案したり、意見を述べたりする前に、関係者や上司、あるいは先輩の同意を取り付けておくことです。従って、十分に根回しが行われたあとに会議に出された議案は、すでに承認されたようなもので、政治的な理由でもないかぎり、あるいはいきなり社長が入ってきて、反対意見でも唱えないかぎり、すべてはスムーズに承認されるのです。

　大切なことは、この根回しの過程は、すべて非公式に行われるということです。会議の席上での根回しなどということはあり得ません。簡単な根回しなら、オフィスで個人ベースで話し合われることもあるでしょうが、重要なものであれば、休日にゴルフをしたり、一緒に食事をしたりして話をします。

Why don't Japanese change their minds after a decision has been made?

Many Westerners say they understand that the decision-making process is a long one, but Japanese are too stubborn once they've decided upon something. "I wish they were more flexible," they say. "It's odd that they stick to things that were decided years ago without re-evaluating them in terms of current circumstances."

It is true that once something has been decided on, Japanese are very reluctant to change it. But why?

The reason has to do with a process called "*nemawashi*," a word originally used to refer to the transplantation of a plant or tree. It means to dig around the perimeter of the main roots, preserving them and cutting off peripheral roots. "*Nemawashi*" has now come to refer to an important practice in Japanese business culture.

"*Nemawashi*" refers to the practice of seeking agreement from one's boss, those related to the project, and one's superiors, before anything is suggested publicly or opinions are given. After "*nemawashi*" has been completed, the project agenda will be approved when it is presented at a meeting because everyone has already discussed it. This is usually the process, unless political reasons come into play and force the project to be dropped, or the president suddenly comes in and opposes it.

The important thing to note about this process is that it is done completely informally. One never does "*nemawashi*" during a meeting! Simple "*nemawashi*" can probably be done on an individual basis at the office, but important matters are discussed on golf trips or at restaurants.

　大きな決裁の場合は、決裁の段階を追って、何度も根回しを行い、それでも反対する人があれば、第三者を通じて調停を頼んだりします。

　さて、こうした過程を経て最終的に決定されたことをもし変更したら、どのようになるでしょう。それは、根回しに関わったすべての人の期待を裏切ることになります。ですからこれを防ぐためには、最初に費やした以上のエネルギーで、再び状況を変更させるための根回しを行わなければなりません。それには、大変な努力とリスクをともない、場合によっては、その人の信用にまで影響を与えかねないのです。こうした理由により、一度決められたことは簡単には変更できないのです。

　この根回しのプロセスを外国人が知らないために、日本人との間で、もう一つ重大な行き違いが生じることがあります。というのも、外国人は会議の場を利用して、提案を行い、そこで討議しようとします。ところが、日本側は根回しのない状態で、いきなり提案されても戸惑うばかりで、どのように処理してよいか分かりません。

　さらに、日本側は会議の場は討議の場ではなく、根回しのための準備として、あるいは根回し後の確認と承認の場として設定するわけですから、そこで外国から来た人があれこれと言っても、どうにもならないのです。そのことから、外国人は自分たちは疎外されていると失望します。また、人によっては、日本人はいつも日本人だけで陰でこそこそとやっているといって、怒りをあらわにする人もいるかもしれません。

「なぜ正々堂々と意見を戦わせないんだ」と外国人は不思

Big decisions require that many rounds of "*ne-mawashi*" occur at the various decision stages. If someone still objects to the proposal, a third party is asked to mediate.

What would happen if changes were made to something which has been decided through this arduous process? Such changes might let down everyone involved in the "*nemawashi*" who had certain expectations of the project. In order to keep people involved and informed, yet, another "*nemawashi*" would have to be done, requiring even more energy than the first one. Changing plans incurs risk and takes a lot of effort, and in some cases, tarnishes a person's reputation. This is why things are rarely changed once they've been decided.

Since many foreigners are unfamiliar with the idea of "*nemawashi*," misunderstandings can occur. For Westerners, meetings are used to make suggestions and then to discuss them. On the other hand, Japanese can be thrown off by impromptu suggestions which come without "*nemawashi*," because they don't know how to handle the situation.

For Japanese, meetings are not the place for discussions. Rather, they are set up as preparation for "*ne-mawashi*," or for approval and confirmation once the "*nemawashi*" process is over. Therefore, Westerners attending such meetings may say any number of things during such meetings, but to little avail. Obviously, they leave such meetings feeling disappointed because they have been paid little attention. Many of them express anger and feel that Japanese always talk about things amongst themselves without including others.

"Why don't they fight back with their own opin-

議に思います。根回しの微妙なプロセスを知らないために長い間待たされ、そのあげくに決裁の過程からも疎外され、期待通りの結論をもらえなかった外国人は、ただ呆気にとられてしまうのです。そして、言います。「それならば、我々としては再提案をしたい。それを聞いて欲しい」と。でも、もう変更はできないのです。

ions?" foreigners wonder. If they are unaware of the subtle process of "*nemawashi*," they may get irritated with the long wait, feel excluded from the consultation process, and be disappointed with the result. They may come back with new approaches, such as, "If that's the way it is, then we'd like to make another suggestion. We want you to listen to it." But usually by that time it is too late and changes are no longer possible.

なぜ日本人は会社にはいってすぐに出世しないの？

　よく、日本人が外国人に自己紹介をするときに困ってしまうのが、相手の名刺に「マネージャー」とか「ディレクター」と書かれているのに、自分の方には何のタイトルもないことです。また、外国人からみても、交渉相手の日本人の立場が分からず、果たしてこの会議に出席する人として適当なのだろうかと疑問に思ってしまいます。

　最近では、外国の事情が分かってきた会社も多くなり、海外用に特別にマネージャーというような肩書を印刷した英語の名刺を用意しているところもありますが、そういう人も、日本国内では肩書のないただの社員だったりするのです。日本の会社では、平社員からその一つ上の肩書をもらうまで、平均10年以上かかるのはごく当たり前のことなのです。

　アメリカなどでは、その人に何らかの仕事が任せられれば、年齢に関係なく、マネージャーの肩書を与えます。マネージャーを日本語にするとき、よく課長などと訳す人がいますが、実際は担当責任者ぐらいに考えておけばよいのではないでしょうか。というのも、日本と欧米では、タイトルに関する考え方そのものが違うのです。

　まず、欧米には、日本にあるような年功による評価システムは存在しません。日本では会社に入社して、すでに10年以上経過して、会社の中でもかなり責任のある仕事をこなしている人でも何の肩書もない人はたくさんいます。多くの場合、どんなに仕事をこなしていても、ある年齢に至らないとそれ相応のタイトルはもらえないのです。

　まして、ディレクターをもし部長と翻訳した場合、欧米ではごく当たり前の30代のディレクターが、日本の大きな会社にどれだけいるかとなると、それは極めて稀な例とい

5 Why aren't Japanese promoted soon after joining a company?

Japanese are often embarrassed when they introduce themselves to foreigners because their business cards contain no titles, whereas the other person's card has "manager" or "director" printed on it. As a result, Westerners aren't sure of their Japanese counterpart's position and wonder if he or she is really the right person to participate in the discussion.

Recently, Japanese companies are becoming sensitive to other countries' conditions. Some now have English business cards with "manager" printed on them just for use with foreigners. However, these people are just ordinary employees with no titles in Japan. Everyone knows that it takes more than ten years for the average employee to receive the first promotion.

In America a person is given the title of "manager" if he or she can handle a certain level of work, regardless of age. When "manager" is translated into Japanese, it usually becomes "*kachō*." In reality, this just means "the person in charge." Japan and the West have different ways of thinking about titles.

The West doesn't have the kind of age-based system of evaluation Japan does. In Japan, many people who have been with the same company for more than ten years do important work yet remain without a title. In most cases, regardless of what kind of work you're doing, you don't receive an official title until you reach a certain age.

Sometimes "director" is translated as "*buchō*." In the West, it is common to find a director who is only in his or her thirties, but this is extremely rare in large

えるのではないでしょうか。日本では部長に昇格するのは、ほとんどの場合40代に入ってからなのです。

　最近でこそ、不況などの影響でかなり変わってきたとはいえ、それでも日本の大手企業では終身雇用を常識として人を雇っています。終身雇用という実に長い年月に亘った個人と会社との関係の中で、その個人は仕事のプロになる以上に、会社のプロとなっていきます。

　すなわち、大きな会社に勤める日本人は、会社が与えてくれる仕事をどのようにこなし、会社の中で人間関係とネットワークをどのように構築し、その会社の業務全体にいかに精通してゆくかということに重きをおくのです。実際日本の企業には本人の専門領域とは関係なく、社内で異動させ、より多くの部門の仕事を覚えてもらうようなローテーション・システムを採用しているところが相当あります。

　従って、日本人が自己紹介をするときには、必ず○○会社の△△ですといって相手に名乗ります。エンジニアの○○ですとか、マーケティングの○○ですというような名乗り方をすることはあまりありません。

　こうした環境の中では、即座に昇進する必要はまったくないのです。時間をかけ、ゆっくりと会社の社風や業務内容を勉強し、かつ自らのキャリアだけでなく、長く会社に忠誠を尽くし、これからも会社と一緒に活動していけると会社側も自分も認識したころはじめて、最初の昇進となるのです。

　しかも、すでにお話したように、日本では年齢そのものが昇進に大きな影響を及ぼします。大学を卒業して、会社に入り、それから何十年もその会社で過ごします。そうした同年齢の人たちが次から次へと会社に入社し、年齢に応じて、すなわち会社に何年長くいたかに応じて、地位が上

Japanese companies, where normally people who are promoted to the director position are in their forties.

Although the situation has changed recently because of the economic recession, large Japanese companies typically hire for lifetime employment. During the long relationship between individual and company, the employee becomes a "pro" at the company rather than a "pro" at a particular job.

For employees of large companies, it is most important to do the work the company gives them, build a network of relationships in the company, and become well-informed about all aspects of the company's business. Actually, Japanese companies utilize a system of rotating employees within the company so that they can learn the operation of many departments. This is unrelated to the employee's area of expertise.

This is why a Japanese introduces him- or herself by giving his name as "so-and-so of such-and-such a company." Rarely would one introduce oneself as "so-and-so of Engineering" or "so-and-so of Marketing."

In this kind of environment there is no necessity for immediate promotion. Japanese spend a long time learning the company's culture and business. They are not just pursuing their own career, but also being loyal to the company. The first promotion comes only after mutual recognition by employee and company that they are able to continue working together for a long time.

As we have seen, age itself is a big factor in promotions. In Japan, people graduate from college, join a company and spend decades there. People enter the company at the same age—typically twenty-two—every year. They are promoted in rank according to the

がっていくのです。

　最近では、こうした年功序列制度や終身雇用制度に疑問を持つ会社も増えてきて、外から優秀な人をヘッドハンティングして、重要な地位につけたりするケースもでてきました。しかし、その場合でさえ、優秀であっても、30代の前半ぐらいまでは別の会社からお呼びのかかるケースはほとんどありません。

　会社を移る場合でも、前の会社に何年ぐらいいて、そこでどれだけ信頼されていたかが、次の会社でのキャリアに大きな影響を与えています。自らのキャリアを磨き、その業種のプロとしてどんどん会社を移ることも良しとする欧米の常識とは、かなり違う常識が、日本の中にはあります。

length of time they have been with the company—that is, according to their age.

Japanese firms are increasingly beginning to question the traditional systems of seniority-based promotion and lifetime employment. We see more and more cases of companies headhunting excellent people from outside for important positions. Even so, it is rare that these top-notch people are recruited by another company once they reach their early thirties.

Even when people change jobs, the amount of time they were at their previous companies and how much they were trusted will greatly influence their new careers. This is quite different from the West, where it is common practice to spruce up one's resumé by changing companies to build expertise in a particular area.

**6 なぜ日本人の上司は
部下のプライバシーにまで頭をつっこむの?**

　以前、日系企業に勤めていたあるアメリカ人が、日本人はどうして部下のプライバシーにまでかかわろうとするのだろうと不満をこぼしたことがありました。

　そのアメリカ人は入社して間もなく、上司に夕食に誘われ、ガールフレンドはいるのか、いつ結婚するつもりなのかなどといった質問にはじまって、今家賃はいくら払っているんだと聞かれ、しかたなくそれに答えると、「そんな高いところに住むなんて若い君にしては贅沢だよ。若いころはもっと苦労しなければ出世できないよ」と注意されたというのです。

　彼は思いました。「そんなことあなたの知ったことじゃないでしょう。私個人の問題なんだから。第一、あなたは今僕が何も苦労していないって思っているんですか。文化も風習も違う日本の会社に就職しているのに」と。

　確かに、欧米に比べて、日本ではビジネスとプライベートとの区別が曖昧なようです。そして、特に上司や年輩社員は、若手社員のプライバシーにどんどんはいりこみます。これは、ビジネスと個人の生活をきちっと区別する欧米の人からみれば、大変失礼な行動に映るのです。

　しかし、日本人にはそれなりの理由があるのです。その理由を知るために、日本での上司と部下との関係に目を向けてみましょう。日本でのビジネスにおける人間関係の中で、最も気を付けなければならないのは、いうまでもなく、自らの直属の上司との関係です。

　上司は先輩として最も尊敬されなければならない人物です。特に終身雇用を常識としている大企業では、上司との人間関係はどちらかが退職するまで続くわけですから、いかにそれが親密なつながりであるか想像できるはずです。

6 **Why do Japanese bosses meddle in the private affairs of their subordinates?**

An American who worked in a Japanese company complained about Japanese supervisors interfering with the private affairs of their subordinates.

Shortly after he started working at a Japanese company, his boss invited him out to dinner, where he asked him if he had a girlfriend and when he planned to get married. Then, when he answered a question about how much rent he was paying, his boss admonished him. "Living in such an expensive place is a luxury for a young guy like you. When you're young you should suffer, or you won't succeed." The American remembered thinking this was none of his boss's business. "It's my problem, not his. I'm suffering plenty already by working at a Japanese company in a completely unfamiliar environment."

In Japan, there is a thin line between business and private matters. "*Sempai*" (more senior employees) and supervisors readily invade the privacy of young employees. Westerners who keep their personal lives separate from their work lives think this is very intrusive.

Of course, Japanese have their own reasons for this. These become obvious when looking at the superior-subordinate relationship. In Japan, it is considered natural that one should make every effort to look after the relationship between oneself and one's immediate boss.

The boss, as a "*sempai*," should be given the utmost respect. This is especially true in large Japanese companies that have lifetime employment. Imagine the intimacy of this connection, where the relationship with one's boss continues until the person retires.

　もちろん、長い年月の間には人事異動があったり、海外へ駐在したり、国内で地方の支社に配置替えになったりということもよくおきます。しかし、そうした後でも、多くの場合、上司は先輩としてその社員との親密な人間関係を維持してゆくのです。

　日本では、往々にして上司はあたかも家族の長のような立場で部内をマネージします（小売り業やファッション業界などで少しずつ変わってきているとはいえ、それでもまだ日本企業では上司の多くは男性なのです）。仕事ができて、優秀な上司とは、部下から親や兄のように慕われる上司を意味しており、特に若い部下は、上司の仕事ぶりをみながらプロフェッショナルとして成長してゆきます。こうした上下関係の中では、上司は部下の個人的な問題にまで立ち入ることはそれほど失礼なことではないのです。

　日本の上司は時には部下に結婚の相手を紹介し、結婚式では仲人の役割を担ったり、さらに若い社員に対しては、生活態度を戒めたりといった指導までします。

　部下をよくマネージできる上司が、社内では能力のある上司とみなされ、その上司本人のさらなる出世にも影響をあたえるのです。従って、もし部下が大きなミスをおかしたり、不幸にして犯罪などを犯してしまった場合、部下と共に上司にも責任が及ぶこともよくあります。不祥事が起きると、その上司はあたかも子供の教育を怠った親のような評価を受け、そのことによってリーダーとしての資質に疑問ありとされるのです。

　ただ、最近こうした日本の伝統的な上下関係が変化してきました。特に裕福でより自由な環境に育った若い世代の社員たちが、こうした上下関係を古い関係として軽視し、

Naturally, over the years, various events such as personnel transfers, overseas postings, and transfers to local branches within Japan occur. The boss, as "*sempai*," often continues to maintain a close relationship with the employee even after any or all of these events have occurred.

The boss often manages his department as if it were a family and he were the head (most bosses are still male in major Japanese companies, although this is slowly changing, especially in certain industries such as retail or fashion). An excellent boss is someone who is admired by his subordinates as an older brother or parental figure. Younger department members develop as professionals by observing their boss's work habits. In this context, it is not so out of line for a boss to get involved in his subordinates' personal affairs.

A Japanese supervisor will even introduce a prospective marriage partner to a subordinate and play the role of the go-between during the marriage ceremony. With younger employees, the boss goes so far as to teach them how to get along in daily life.

The boss who can manage his subordinates well is seen by the company as a capable superior. His ability to manage his department smoothly affects his future promotions. If a subordinate makes a big mistake, or in the unfortunate case where he or she commits a crime, often both boss and the subordinate take responsibility for it. When a negative incident occurs, the boss is treated as if he or she were a parent who neglected his child's upbringing. As such, doubts about his qualifications as a leader surface.

This traditional type of supervisor/subordinate relationship is beginning to appear less nowadays. Younger employees brought up in a more economically affluent

もっとビジネスライクな付き合いを求めるようになってき
ているのです。

　しかも、若者の間では、終身雇用の価値観自体が揺らい
できており、仕事が面白くなければ転職すると答える若者
の数が目立ってくるようになりました。そうした若者はた
だ上司であるというだけでは、上司についてはゆかなくな
ってきたのです。
　こうした、新しい価値観の中で、日本企業の社風がどう
変化してゆくか。特に古い世代に属する40代以上の「先輩」
たちは、若者のそうした動きを不安そうに眺めているよう
です。

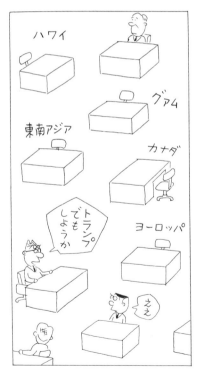

and liberal atmosphere don't take this kind of relationship as seriously, seeing it as the "old" way of relating. There is increasing preference for more "business-like" associations.

In fact, the system of lifetime employment itself is being questioned by young people themselves, and many more say they would take another job if their work was no longer interesting. These young people no longer follow their boss unconditionally just because he is the boss.

Given these new customs and values, how will the organization of large Japanese companies change? The over-forty "*sempai*" of the older generation seem to feel very uncomfortable with the attitudes of young employees.

なぜ日本の会社は責任領域が曖昧なの？

「アメリカ人にミスを指摘すると、すぐ言い訳をして、これは私の責任ではありません、なんていいますよね。これには本当に腹が立ちますよ」。アメリカに駐在する日本人にアメリカ人の部下のことを聞けば、ほとんどの人がこのように答えます。

これに対して、アメリカ人は言います。「日本人ってコミュニケーションの仕方も曖昧ならば、仕事の責任領域も曖昧ですね。だから、私はどのようにして会社に貢献したらいいのか分からなくなることがあるのです」

日本の会社では、会社の仕事はみんなで共同して成し遂げ、責任もグループ全体でとってゆこうとします。ですから、個々の守備範囲はおおまかにはありますが、それは絶対ではありません。グループでコンセンサスをとって、すべての人の了解の元にプロジェクトを前進させ、外部からの問い合わせや苦情にも、会社として対応してゆきます。人が気付かなかったことを進んでカバーし、部下のミスを自分のミスとして共同で修正してゆく態度がよい態度として賞賛されるのです。

アメリカの職場は、もっと契約的です。個人が自ら持つ技量を会社に提示し、そして決められた仕事を成し遂げるためにその会社に雇われるわけですから、個々の職域が明快に規定されることになります。そして、その職域での功績に従って、昇進や昇給が決定されます。

従って、アメリカの職場では自らの領域をしっかりと守ろうとします。何かミスがあった場合でも、それが自分自身の間違いでなく、ボスの指示が曖昧だったことが原因だ

Why are areas of responsibility unclear in Japanese companies?

"When I point out an American's mistake, he immediately makes an excuse and says it's not his responsibility! It makes me so angry!" Almost all Japanese working in the U.S. with American subordinates respond in this way if you ask them about attitudes towards responsibility.

Americans would respond "The Japanese way of communicating is too vague. Not only that, the boundaries of responsibility are ambiguous, too. I find it difficult to see how I'm supposed to make a contribution to the company."

In Japanese companies, everyone works together to accomplish the company's goals, and the entire group takes responsibility. Areas of individual responsibility do exist, but they are largely undefined. Group consensus is sought, and projects are advanced on this basis. Questions and complaints from outside are dealt with by the company as a whole. Praise is given to those who catch previously undetected problems and correct the mistakes of subordinates; a good boss will take responsibility for mistakes and correct them with the help of others.

The relationship of American workers with their companies is more contractual. Job applicants present themselves to the company as having a particular skill set, and they are hired to accomplish certain tasks. The area of individual responsibility is clearly determined. Promotions and pay raises are determined based upon outstanding achievement within that area.

In America, one must protect one's work domain. In order to preserve professional standing, when a mistake is made that is not one's own fault, an employee doesn't

ったりすれば、自らのプロとしての立場を守るために相手が上司といえども抗議をすることを怠りません。これを日本人は言い訳をするといって嫌うのです。

　ここにも、和を保つために謝る日本社会と、「インディビジュアリズム」に根ざしたアメリカ流のプロフェッショナリズムといった価値観の違いからくる誤解があるのです。

　「だまって謝ればいいものを、言い訳をするなんて」と思う日本人に対して、アメリカ人は「この仕事は私のプロとしての将来にかかわるものだから、不当なことを言われたり、自分の担当領域でないことまで責任を持たされたりすれば、理路整然と抗議するのは当然の権利」という風になるのです。

　アメリカ人は、過ちを認めることは、自らのプロとしての質の低さを認めることになり、そのことが次の昇進などにも影響し、さらには個人としてのキャリアにもひびが入ると思っているわけですから、真剣になって当然なのです。これは、問題があればグループ全体で受けとめてゆこうとする日本人にとっては最も理解しにくいことといえるでしょう。

　グループ思考と、個人思考。そのどちらにも長所もあれば、短所もあるでしょう。最近アメリカでは、責任分担があまりにも明快に分かれすぎていることからくる弊害が云々されています。例えば、異なる責任領域の中間にある仕事を無視したり、または実はしっかりと反省して、対策を練らなければいけないようなミスを見逃してしまったりといったことです。逆に日本では、個人としての責任が明快でないために、リーダーシップが発揮しにくく、決裁にも時間がかかりすぎることへの批判をよく聞きます。

hesitate to protest to his boss that the cause may be somewhere else, or that instructions were unclear. Japanese see this type of behavior as inappropriate self-justification.

Misunderstandings often arise from value differences between Japanese and American society. In Japan, people apologize for the sake of preserving group harmony. In America, the sense of professionalism is informed by a deep-seated "individualism."

Japanese think, "I'll just apologize and refrain from making excuses…." Americans think, "Since this job is part of my professional path to the future, if someone accuses me unjustly or holds me responsible for something that was not part of my job, I have a natural right to protest clearly and logically."

Americans feel that to admit a mistake is to acknowledge a deficiency in their professional skill, which would affect their next promotion and jeopardize their personal career. Naturally, they take mistakes very seriously. This is hard for Japanese to understand, since they take responsibility as a group whenever there is a problem.

Both group-oriented thinking and individual-oriented thinking have their respective strengths and weaknesses. Recently, people in America think that dividing up work responsibilities too much can create negative side effects: people may ignore vital tasks that fall into the gaps between different job descriptions, or fail to acknowledge real errors that need to be analyzed and corrected. Conversely, since individual responsibility is vague in Japan, it is not uncommon to hear the criticisms even amongst Japanese themselves that leadership skills don't get the chance to develop, accountability is

　責任に関するこうした考え方の違いは、それぞれの文化の最も深いところに根ざしたものだけに、そう簡単に両者を融合させることもできません。しかし、あえて双方の長所をとり入れてゆくことが、効率的な職場造りをする上で必要なことではないでしょうか。

vague, and decision-making takes far too much time.

It would be best to build a work environment that fully incorporates the best traits of both ways of thinking. Underlying cultural differences in perceptions about responsibility, however, make it quite hard to integrate them.

8 なぜ日本人はいつまでも同じチームに
いようとするの？

　終身雇用の職場で働き、上司や先輩との長い人間関係の
中で生きる日本人をアメリカ人がみるときに、不思議に思
うことがあります。

　それは、理不尽にすら思える日本人の腰の重さです。な
ぜ日本人は、チャンスがあちこちにあるのに、常に同じ場
所、同じ職場にいようとするのでしょう。そして、なぜ日
本人は我慢することを美徳とするのでしょう。納得がいか
なければ仕事を移り、人生の方向だって自分の思うように
変えていくことが、なぜ彼らにはできないのでしょうか。

　一般に、アメリカ人は人と人との集まりをチームとして
捉えます。この考え方を代表するものがプロ野球ではない
でしょうか。そこでは、選手の守備範囲が決まっていて、
それに応じてチームのためにやらなければならない義務も
限定されます。守備範囲の中間に球がやってくれば、お互
いにどちらがボールをとるか声をかけ合い、確認をしてか
ら対処します。しかも、チームの目標は優勝することです
から、苦労の末優勝を勝ち得れば、みんなで抱き合ってそ
れを喜びます。ところが、シーズンが終われば、選手はよ
り条件の良いチームがあればそこに移動し、過去のチーム
での友情や連帯は忘れたかのように、新しいチームで頑張
ります。

　これに対して、日本での人と人との集まり方は、相撲に
代表されます。相撲は、入門した時から長い時間をかけて
同じ部屋で訓練を受けます。シーズンが終わっても、その
部屋の中から出ることもなく、親方を親のように思いなが
ら、あるいは先輩の力士に召し使いのように仕えながら、
時間をかけて相撲を覚え、毎日訓練をします。理不尽に思
えることがあっても公に文句を言うことはありません。そ
こで耐えてゆくことも、一つの鍛錬であると解釈されます。

8 Why do Japanese tend to stay with the same group?

Americans often express curiosity and surprize about the Japanese traditions of lifetime employment and long-term relationships with bosses and mentors.

This immobility strikes them as unreasonable. Why do Japanese tend to stay with the same job, even though other opportunities arise? Why do they think patience is always a virtue? Why can't they change jobs and lifestyles if things aren't going well?

Americans generally think of a group of people as a team. Professional baseball provides a good example. A player has his own area to field, which regulates his duties on the team. If a ball is hit between two players' fielding ranges, they confirm vocally who will get it. Of course, the goal of the team is to win, and everyone celebrates and hugs each other when a hard-fought victory is achieved. But when the season ends, a player may well go to a different team if it offers better contract terms. And he'll play hard for the new team, setting aside his friendships and solidarity with the previous team.

The Japanese style of group behavior, on the other hand, is best represented by sumo. After apprentices enter a training stable, they stay there for a long time. Even when the season ends, they don't change stables. They view their stablemaster as a parent, and serve their mentors slavishly. They devote a long time to learning their sport, and practice daily. They don't complain openly, even when something is unreasonable. Endurance is considered part of the training. In return, the stable

その部屋こそは、力士が引退するまでお世話になる場所で、うまく出世できれば、その部屋を継ぐか、あるいはその功績で、さらに大きなグループである相撲協会から新たな部屋をもつ機会が与えられます。

この野球と相撲との違いが、そのまま職場でのものの考え方や、そこに働く人々の意識の中にも見て取れます。

日本人からみれば、アメリカ人は常に自らの仕事の守備範囲を意識し、それに過敏になり過ぎているように思えます。そして、プロジェクトが終われば、あたかもそれまで培った人間関係なんてなかったかのように、さっさとよそに行ってしまうので、なんてビジネスライクな人たちなんだろうと残念に思ったりするのです。

実際に、一つの製品が完成した後に、日本の顧客がアフターサービスを求めて、アメリカ側の製品開発や契約交渉の担当者だった人に問い合わせても、それはもう私の責任ではないと言われたり、そのプロジェクト・チーム自体が解散してしまっているといった苦情をよく聞きます。でも、アメリカ人にしてみれば、それならなぜ日本側は、最初からニーズをちゃんと主張しなかったんだと批判します。分かっていれば、予算が許す限り顧客サービスのためのシステムを充実したり、例えばオンラインで苦情を処理する方法を考案したりできるのにというのです。

「いや、システムの問題じゃないんだよ。人と人との付き合いの問題なんだ。そうした心がけこそ顧客が最も要求するものなんだよ」

日本人のこの反論をアメリカの人に分かってもらうことは困難でしょう。それは、常に同じグループに帰属することを良しとする日本人の心理を、自らに合ったチームを渡り歩くアメリカ人に押しつけるようなもので、アメリカ人からしてみれば、そうした主張は合理性に欠け、ビジネス

takes care of them until they retire. If they get promoted and do well, they will eventually take over the stable, or are given the chance to set up a new stable by the Sumo Association, an even bigger group unto itself.

The difference between being a member of an American-style baseball team and being part of a Japanese sumo stable can also be seen in the differing workplace and work mentalities of Americans and Japanese.

From the Japanese standpoint, Americans are too conscious about protecting the boundaries of their areas of responsibility. Americans seem somewhat distant in that they move on to other things once a project is done, almost as if no interpersonal relationships developed over the course of the project.

In fact, I've heard many complaints from Japanese who have contacted the person in charge of product development or contract negotiations for after-sale service—only to be told that it is no longer his responsibility and the team disbanded after the project's completion. For their part, Americans criticize Japanese for not clarifying their needs at the beginning. If only they had done this, they say, they could have set up a better system for customer service—an on-line system to manage complaints, for example.

"It's not only a question of the system. It's a matter of relationships. That's what customers want most," the Japanese would say.

Americans have a hard time understanding this way of thinking. It seems like a kind of forced togetherness for Americans, who look for the best match between their career goals and the needs of a particular team. The Japanese mentality values belonging to the same group

上からも効率的であるとはみなされません。

　この両者の意識の違いは、下手をすると双方への不信感へと発展するリスクをともないます。お互いに良いチームワークをと思っても、このようにチームワークに関する根本的な考え方に違いがあるわけですから大変です。恒久的な人間関係の上にビジネスを構築しようとする日本人。そして、チームをその時の業務だけのためのチームとして捉え、顧客といえども対等に自らの立場を主張してくるアメリカ人。この行き違いは思った以上に深刻な誤解へと発展してしまうのです。

almost regardless of these other factors. Americans feel the Japanese way is irrational and inefficient.

These different approaches give rise to the risk of distrust between the two sides. Even though both sides say they want good teamwork, there's a basic difference in what good teamwork looks like to them. Japanese try to do business on the basis of long-term interpersonal relationships. Americans see a team as a group of people working together on a particular project. This difference lies behind many more serious misunderstandings than one might think.

9 なぜ日本人にとって「お客様は神様」なの？

　日本人が「お客様は神様だ」というと、なんだって、彼らだって人間だろうとアメリカ人は反論します。下らない反論のための反論だと思わないでください。この反論の中には、アメリカ人と日本人のビジネスに対する意識の違いが隠されているのです。

　当然、アメリカ人にとっても顧客は大切です。アメリカ人もできる限り顧客の要望を考慮し、より顧客が満足するサービスを提供しようと努力します。しかし、それでもアメリカ人は考えます。顧客は人間で、人間であるならば、我々と平等に取り扱われるべきだと。アメリカでの顧客との関係は、互いに「パートナーシップ」にあると言えるほど、対等なビジネス上の関係なのです。

　アメリカ人には、日本式の顧客との関係が不思議でたまりません。長い時間やエネルギーをかけて、時にはお金まで浪費して、それははたして意味があるのだろうか。「もっと別の顧客がすぐに商談にのってくれるかもしれない。もっといい見返りをくれる顧客を探した方がいいんじゃないか。なぜ日本人はそうした顧客を見つけようとしないんだ？　ビジネスはビジネス。もっと利益を中心に合理的にできないんだろうか」とアメリカ人は思うのです。

　お互いに利害が一致すれば、まず仕事を一緒にしようというのがアメリカ人のスタンスですから、お互いに誤解があったり、後で問題が起きないように、まず契約書を交換しようとします。それは、相手に対して不信感があるからではなく、契約書を交わすことによって、仕事を前進させ

9 Why do Japanese say "The customer is God"?

Americans don't understand the Japanese saying that "The customer is God." They feel that customers are just human beings. Although these may seem like mere harmless statements, they betray important differences in the way Americans and Japanese do business.

Naturally, customers are very important to Americans. They try to take the customer's needs into account, making an effort to give satisfying service. However, Americans believe that since customers are only human, everyone should be treated equally. The relationship between customer and supplier is a relatively equal business relationship, even to the point where it is possible to speak of a "partnership" between the two.

They question the efficiency of the Japanese process of taking a long time to build a relationship with a customer. Is it worth getting a customer if it means that time, energy and even money are wasted in the process?

Americans often feel doubts about the Japanese way of doing business. They say, "Well, another customer will come along soon. It's better to find a customer who's willing to sign a contract quickly. Why don't Japanese try to find these kinds of customers? Business is business. Why can't they do things more rationally and focus more on profits?"

The American stance is that providing people agree to something of mutual interest and benefit, they should work together. Americans want to sign a contract at the very start to avoid problems arising from misunderstandings—not because they don't trust their business

るための基本事項を明確にしたいということなのです。しかし、人間関係を優先する日本で、もし契約の話を最初から持ち出すと、逆に相手への不信感のあらわれと誤解されたり、すぐにお金が欲しいための工作だと思われたりする可能性があるのです。

こうした契約に基づいて仕事をするアメリカでは、もし、その後に顧客の事情で納期に変更が生じたり、顧客からの情報提供が遅れたために、サービスが遅延したりした場合は、その時の調整を顧客に対しても遠慮なく対等な立場で行うことを常とします。

すなわち、顧客が至急の仕事を要求する場合は、その分だけ特別な支払いをすることは当然ですし、顧客の事情で何か問題が起きた時は、その責任を顧客がとることも常識なのです。

そんなアメリカ人が、顧客が神様として「そこをなんとか頼みますよ」といったときに、「うーん分かりました。いつもお世話になっていますから」と、ご無理ごもっともの対応をする日本人をみると、「この日本のビジネスマンはなんでも顧客のいいなりになっているぞ。なんて弱い人間なんだ」と思ってしまうのです。

しかし、日本人の考え方は違います。顧客の無理を聞けば、次に顧客とよりよい人間関係が築けるわけで、一度固い信頼関係が構築されれば、その顧客は半永久的に物やサービスを買ってくれると考えます。もちつもたれつの関係ができあがるのです。「あれだけ努力してくれたから」とか「何度も足を運んでくれたから」といって、顧客はセールスをする人の熱意にほだされてゆくのです。熱意を見せ、努力していることを理解してもらうことは、日本では商品の質と同じくらい大切なセールステクニックといっても過言ではないのです。

partners, but because by signing a contract they'll instantly create mutual trust. In Japan, the relationship is given priority, so if negotiations immediately begin with a contract, the assumption will be that there is a lack of trust or that it's a ploy to get money fast.

In America, if there's a change in the delivery date due to extenuating circumstances with the client, or if service is delayed due to customer lateness in supplying information, the supplier can make adjustments vis-a-vis the customer from a position of equality because a contract exists. In other words, if the client requests a rush job, the supplier can naturally charge separately for it. It's generally understood that the customer will take responsibility for problems caused by changes in his own situation. Americans don't understand it when the Japanese customer, as God, says to the Japanese supplier "I want you to get this done for me at all costs" and the supplier responds "Yes, I understand. I am indebted to you always." An American seeing this will think, "This Japanese businessman is his customer's flunkey. What weak person."

Japanese see it differently. When a customer makes an unreasonable request, trying to meet it is an opportunity to build an even better relationship. Once a solid relationship is built, that customer will continue buying services or products almost indefinitely. It becomes a "You-scratch-my-back-and-I'll-scratch-yours" kind of relationship. The customer is impressed by the salesperson's diligence. "He took all that trouble on my behalf," he thinks, or, "He came to visit me so many times." It's not an overstatement to say that eagerness and making the customer aware of your efforts is a sales technique as important as the quality of the goods themselves.

　そして特に日本の顧客は、売り手がどれだけ熱心に仕事に取り組んでくれるかを見極めるために、最初は小さなオーダーを出して、それをいかに完璧な形で納品してくれるかを確かめることがあります。こんなとき、ミスがあれば、そのダメージを克服するのは大変です。

　納期を守ること。商品自体ではなくそのパッケージまで気を配り、書類もきちんと整えること。そして、納品後のアフターサービスの努力を怠らないこと。さらに何にもまして、具体的な用事がたとえなくても頻繁に顧客を訪ね、業界の情報を提供したり、顧客のためになる資料を提出したり、時には夜食事に招待したりすること。これらの行為があってはじめて、顧客と良いビジネス・リレーションを造ることができるのです。

　そして、一度ビジネス・リレーションができあがれば、日本の顧客は実によくその関係を尊重します。顧客がその関係を裏切れば、日本の商習慣からみて、その顧客自体の信用にも影響を与えることがあるからです。これは、上下の関係のようでもありますが、実は公平で相互的でもあるのです。努力をして努力を認める。こうした生臭い人間関係が、「お客様は神様です」といった考え方の背景にはあるのです。

Japanese customers judge suppliers by the extent to and enthusiasm with which they take on their work. Therefore, the first order they place place is small, to confirm that the seller will deliver the goods in perfect condition. Since this is the first order, it's extremely difficult to compensate for any loss of reputation that may be caused by mistakes. This includes maintaining the delivery schedule and paying attention not just to the goods themselves, but to the packaging as well. The paperwork must also be prepared properly and with due courtesy, and effort must be made to provide service after delivery. Beyond that, even with no specific business at hand, the supplier will often visit the customer, offering him information about the industry, resources, or materials that may be of use. At times, he might even take him out for dinner. These kinds of actions forge good business relationships.

Once relationships are established, Japanese customers will do their best to honor them. According to Japanese business custom, once a customer betrays this relationship, it impacts the credibility of the customer himself. Effort is made, acknowledged and appreciated. This is the complex web of interaction behind the Japanese mentality that "The customer is God."

10 なぜ日本人は人を叱ってばかりいるの？

　日系企業で働く欧米の人にとって耐えられないほどつらいことがあります。それは、日本人が自分の業績を誉めてくれないことです。それどころか、自分としては良い仕事をしているつもりなのに叱られたりします。そして、こうしたことが積み重なって、せっかく入社した日本の会社を早々に辞めたりといったケースが続出しているのです。いったいどこがどのようにすれ違ってしまったのでしょうか。

　この背景には、日本と欧米の間でのマネージメントに関する哲学の違いがあるのです。欧米では、部下が良い仕事をすれば即座に口頭で誉め、うまく行かなかった場合でも、それに対して具体的なフィードバックを与えるのが良いこととされています。こうしたフィードバックは、直接本人に対して行うのが常で、部下は口頭での評価をもらうことで、さらに良い仕事をしようとするのです。

　非公式に与えられるフィードバックやまた公式に与えられる評価は、当然その後の昇給や昇進について会社と話し合うときに、その人の価値を定める上での証拠となるわけですから、上司からのこうしたコメントの持つ意味は大変大きなものであるといえましょう。

　日本では部下の職域を事細かに定めて、それに従った評価を行ったりはしません。個人はグループの中に混ざっているわけで、上司との長い人間関係を構築してゆく中で、特に一つ一つを口頭で確認しなくても社員間の信頼関係は充分に培われているわけです。むしろ、それを敢えて確かめようとすると、逆に信頼関係を疑っているのではと思われたりすることすらあるようです。

　しかも、日本には叱咤激励という言葉があるように、上

10 Why do Japanese bosses reprimand their subordinates?

One thing that Westerners working in Japanese companies find hard to tolerate is that Japanese seldom if ever
praise their work. Even worse, they may get criticism
despite all their effort. Frustration mounts, and foreigners in Japanese companies often end up quitting quite
soon. What signals are getting crossed between Western
employees and Japanese employers?

Japan and the West have a fundamental difference in
business philosophy. In the West, managers are trained
to praise subordinates on the spot when a job is well
done, and to offer constructive feedback if something
goes wrong. It is typical for a manager to give this kind
of feedback directly to the subordinate, and it is through
this kind of ongoing dialogue that employees are moti-
vated and their performance improves.

Feedback given both informally and in performance
appraisals naturally leads to discussions about wage
increases and promotions, which may provide further
evidence that the company values an employee. The
manager's assessment carries considerable weight.

In Japan, employees aren't evaluated according to a
carefully determined work field. Rather, individuals are
part of a group, so unspoken trust should develop in the
process of building a long-term relationship with one's
boss. If an individual takes the risk of verbally confirm-
ing his or her own progress, it may have the opposite
effect of appearing to call that trust into question.

The will to work and learn is instilled in subordinates

司は部下にあえて厳しい言葉をかけることによって、やる気を起こしてもらおうとしたりします。叱られなくなったらおしまいだという言葉があるように、日本では、上司はちょうど親が子供を叱ることによって一人前の大人に育てるように、部下に、特に若い部下には厳しく接することもあるのです。これは正に「愛の鞭」で、上司と部下との間に信頼関係があればあるほど、この「愛の鞭」によって、上司は自らのノウハウを部下に習得してもらおうとするのです。

この「愛の鞭」を欧米の人は誤解するのです。ビジネスの世界において、言葉のメッセージを解釈せずにそのままの形で捉える習慣がある彼らは、厳しい言葉をかけられれば、それはそのまま自分が低く評価されていると思ってしまうのです。

誉められることはほとんどなく、たまに何か言われるときはネガティブなコメントしか返ってこないので、欧米人は不安になり、時には怒りさえおぼえるのです。そして、自分はちゃんと仕事をしてきたと思っているわけですから、自らの立場を守ろうと、上司に反論したり、自分の立場を説明しようとしたりします。しかし、叱咤激励をされているときは、ただ黙ってそれを「はい」といって受けることが良しとされている日本人からみると、この欧米の人々の自己主張の意味が分からず、なんて横着で横柄な連中だということになってしまうのです。

欧米、特にアメリカでは、例え部下に注意を与えたいときでも、まずはその人の良いところを誉めるように心がけます。良いところを評価し、それから問題点を指摘するのです。そしてその後再度良かった点を強調します。こうした、アプローチに慣れているアメリカ人が日本人から厳しく注意されると、何か人格までもが傷つけられたかのようなショックを受けてしまうのです。

through harsh words from their superiors. Japanese use the word shittagekirei. This expression means that if no one bothers to scold you, it's because you are hopeless. So a boss is hard on his subordinates, particularly on the young ones, in the same way that a parent scolds a child in order to help it mature. This is known as the "whip of love," and a boss uses it to help his staff acquire company know-how. The closer the relationship between boss and subordinate, the more he may use it.

Westerners often misunderstand this "whip of love." In the business world, they tend to take words at face value, so if harsh words are used they assume they're being negatively evaluated.

Westerners at Japanese companies are almost never praised. If their boss does say something, it is usually negative. They become insecure and hurt, and a vicious cycle ensues. Since they have been doing good work, they try to protect their position by disagreeing with their boss and explaining what they have done. A Japanese subordinate just accepts reprimands silently with a "*hai*" (yes), and usually cannot understand why Westerners try to defend their positions. They often assume that they're being lazy and arrogant.

Westerner managers, particularly Americans, are careful first to praise the subordinate's strengths or accomplishments—even when their basic intention is to caution or reprimand. The approach is first to create a positive context through praise, and then to correct the problem areas. After that the good points are reinforced once again. When Americans accustomed to this kind of

　残念ながら、欧米人の中には、このフィードバックの与え方や評価に関する日本と欧米との常識の狭間で苦しみ、絶望して日本の会社を去っていく人も多いのです。そして、そんな外国人をみて、「だめだなあ。忍耐力がないんだよ。だからアメリカ人には仕事を任せられないんだ」と日本人がコメントします。これはまったく悲しく辛い行き違いなのです。

approach are reprimanded by Japanese, they are shocked and take it quite personally.

Unfortunately, many Westerners who quit Japanese companies do so because of this gulf between different styles of giving feedback and appraising performance. To make matters worse, when Japanese see this kind of foreigner, some say: "He's no good. He's got no endurance. No wonder we can't delegate work to Americans." It is a particularly tragic kind of misunderstanding.

11 なんで日本人はビジネスの国際化というかけ声を大切にするの?

　日本で国際化という言葉が聞かれるようになって、すでに15年、いや20年の月日が経つでしょうか。多少なりとも日本のことを知っている外国人ならば、この国際化という日本語を一度は耳にしたことがあるはずです。

　国際化とは、日本を海外に向けて開かれた、海外と積極的にコミュニケーションができるような国にしようというスローガンです。そして、このスローガンはバブル経済が崩壊した後は、企業が世界で生き残ってゆくためのせっぱ詰まった戦略にまで置き換えられるようになりました。

　この戦略の一部が、英語を話し、海外と交渉できる人材を育成することでした。国際企業では、少し前から、会社案内などのマテリアルを英語で作成したり、海外からの人材やまたは海外でのビジネス経験者を導入して、その企業の海外での活動を促進しようとしたのです。

　しかし、この国際化ということを考えるとき、なんとなくそれがかけ声だけに終始して、みんな国際化を目指すことはいいことだと思っていても、それをどのように実行したらいいのかは分からない、何だか言葉だけが空回りしている、そんな気がしてなりません。

　ですから、外国人が「よし、国際化するんだな」と意気込んで、日本の会社に入社しても、結局は失望してその会社を去っていったり、なんだ国際化なんて結局は言葉だけのことじゃないかと批判して、日本嫌いになってしまったりするケースも多くあります。なぜ、こうしたことが起きるのでしょうか。

　おそらく責任は日本側、そして日本と交流する外国人の双方にあるのではないかと思います。日本側が理解しなければならないことは、国際化とは単に英語が話せる人を雇

What do Japanese mean by internationalization?

The word internationalization has been around for fifteen or twenty years in Japan. If you know a little about Japan, no doubt you've heard the Japanese word for it: "*kokusaika.*"

It's a slogan meant to show that Japan is open to the outside world and can communicate actively and positively with it. In the aftermath of the bursting of Japan's bubble economy, it has become a desperate survival strategy for companies with global ambitions.

Speaking English and fostering employees who can negotiate with foreigners in English is part of this strategy. Large companies learned some time ago to promote their international business activities by creating slick English-language public relations materials and by bringing in foreigners or people with overseas business experience.

However, it seems that a lot of this talk of internationalization is just that—talk. The word "internationalization" itself has become an empty catch-phrase. Everyone aspires to it, but few know how to put it fully into practice.

Westerners who enthusiastically join Japanese companies with the expectation that Japan is "internationalizing" become disillusioned and end up quitting. Sometimes they take extremely negative views of Japan and voice the criticism that internationalization is meaningless there. Why does this happen?

Responsibility lies both with Japan and with the foreigners who interact with them. Japanese must understand that internationalization is not simply a matter of

い、または海外のものをより多く買い、そして書類を英文にすることだけを意味しているのではないということです。相手のビジネス文化を理解する柔軟な心と、違った文化であってもそれを受け入れ、企業の血の中に混ぜてゆく公平さと勇気を持つことが国際化の第一歩なのです。

　国際企業では、外国人をどんどん採用し、本社と交流させ、さらには意思決定にも参加させてゆくことが大切です。相手が自らの文化にそぐわないといって疎外していては、国際化は永遠に達成されません。双方の強い部分を取り出して融合させ、新しい企業文化を創造することが大切なのです。

　また、国際化と西欧化とを取り違えている人も多いようです。国際化したければ、世界のあらゆる人々と平等に付き合い、現地の文化を尊重できるスタンスが必要です。このことを日本人はよく肝に銘じておく必要があります。

　さて、日本が国際化できていないという外国の批判をつきつめてみれば、日本が自分の国のようになっていないという批判に繋がってしまうことがよくあります。自分の国のビジネスの常識、マナー、そしてエチケット。日本人がそれを理解していないからといって批判をするのは公平な態度とはいえません。

　こうした、双方のアプローチが可能になる環境を創造することこそが、究極の国際化のテーマなのではないでしょうか。この章でも示したように、お互いの文化背景が異なっている以上、この課題を実践するためには、いったい問題がどこから来ていて、それがどんな文化背景に基づくの

hiring people who speak English, speaking and writing in English, or buying more foreign goods. The first step to internationalization is having the flexibility of mind to understand the business culture of one's trading partners, then to have the courage and fairness to accept it and allow a cultural blending to take place.

It is very important for Japanese international companies to hire foreigners and let them interact with the home office. Furthermore, they must also be allowed to participate in decision making. If you reject your foreign partner or associate because he is incompatible with your culture, you will never achieve true internationalization. It is vital that you select the strengths of both sides, meld them together, and forge a new company culture based on this mixture.

Many people confuse internationalization with Westernization. If you want to internationalize, you need to have a staff who can interact equally with people from all over the world, and who can respect the local culture of the area they are in. Japanese should take this to heart.

By the same token, if you analyze foreign criticism about Japan's lack of internationalization, you'll find many cases where it stems from some difference between Japan and an other country. At the same time, it is unfair to heap all the blame on Japanese for not fully understanding the etiquette, manners and business values of that different country.

Ultimately, the concept of internationalization means an environment where approaches from various sides are possible. As this chapter shows, in light of cultural differences on both sides, it is necessary to explore the cultural background that is often the basis of misunder-

かということを理解する必要がでてきます。

　こうした地道なプロセスと情報交換、それに基づいた勇気のある改革とがいっしょになって、はじめて海外との生産的で効率的なビジネス環境が構築できるようになるのです。

standings in business approaches.

Japan will be able to conduct productive and efficient business with foreigners once it establishes a steady process of information exchange on the cultural level, and introduces courageous reforms based upon what is learned.

?

第4章
不思議な日本の社会現象

●

CHAPTER 4
Strange Japanese
Social Phenomena

1 なぜ日本人は女性を差別するの？

　日本人は何度この質問を海外の人から受けたことでしょうか。日本は男性優位の社会で、女性の地位は極めて低いという評判はすでに欧米では定着しているようです。さて、それでは実態はどうでしょう。

　残念ながら、女性の差別は歴然と社会の中に残っています。ただ、状況はかなり変わってきています。女性の職場への進出も進んでいますし、政治の世界でも前の衆議院議長が女性だったように、それなりに女性の地位は向上してきています。

　ただ、職種や産業によっては、まだまだ女性は低い地位に甘んじているようです。金融界や商社、さらに製造業などでは女性の管理職はまだまれで、場所によっては未だにアシスタントとしての役割しか担わせてくれません。

　反面、サービス業やメディア関係、あるいは編集プロダクションなどといった中小のビジネスにおいては、最近女性がどんどん進出してくるようになりました。また、教育現場などにも女性が目立ちます。

　従って、欧米のマスコミが報道しているような日本の女性に対するイメージは、多少ステレオタイプな感じがします。ただ、欧米でこのようなイメージが広がる背景には、日本と欧米との文化背景の違いによる誤解も幾分かはあるようです。

　一つは、日本人は外国人に比べ、ビジネスの席でもどんどん人のプライバシーにかかわる質問をします。これは、前にも説明したように、ビジネスを進める前によりよい人間関係を構築したいという日本人の発想によるものですが、そうした背景に基づいて、日本では女性に対しても年齢を聞いたり、夫やボーイフレンドのことを聞いたりします。

Why do Japanese discriminate against women?

Japan is a male-oriented society. Westerners often come to Japan with the notion that Japanese women's status is extremely low, so they often ask the above question. What is the reality?

Unfortunately, discrimination against women clearly still exists in Japanese society. Nevertheless, things are changing. Women are making advances in the workplace and in politics, where the former head of the Diet's lower house was a woman. In many ways, the status of women is improving.

In some professions and industries, however, women's status remains quite low. Female managers are still rare in the financial world and trading companies. Women are only permitted to be assistants at certain manufacturing companies.

The good news is that women have recently been making rapid inroads in service industries, the media, publishing production companies, and small businesses. Women also hold outstanding positions in the education field.

Japanese women are often portrayed in a stereotypical way by the Western media. Behind this image lies a significant cultural misunderstanding.

First of all, Japanese will ask personal questions even in a business environment. As explained earlier, this is a result of the desire to forge good personal relationships before proceeding with business discussions. Japanese will therefore ask a woman about her age, or her husband or boyfriend.

　また、時にはお酒の席などで、「あなたはきれいなのになぜ結婚しないんだい」などと質問する男性もいます。その人の意識を洗い出せば、確かに女性に対する固定したイメージがあるのかもしれません。ただ、その人はだいたいにおいては、その女性と仕事上のよい人間関係を構築しようとしているだけで、それ以上の意味はないわけです。しかし、こうした日本人の行為が、外国から出張してきた女性を憤慨させることは多くあるのです。

　また、日本でも海外で起きているセクハラの問題が話題になってきています。従って、海外に駐在したりする前に、欧米では女性を取り扱うときに特に注意をするようにといったアドバイスを受けて旅立つ人がかなりいます。そこで、外国に着任して、女性に対する対応に過敏に、そして慎重になりすぎて、逆にフレンドリーでないと女性から批判を受けるケースも多いのです。

　多くのアメリカにある日本企業が、女性への差別があったということで、女性の従業員から告訴されていますが、実はそれらのケースの多くが、アメリカ人従業員同士でおきた問題であったということをここで強調しておきましょう。にもかかわらず、そうした事件が表面化したときに、会社側が適切な対応をとらなかったということが、事態を深刻にしてしまったのです。つまり、社内での法律上の闘争に慣れていない日本人のマネージメントが、セクハラの問題への法的な対応を誤ったことが、会社に対する訴訟にまで発展した原因だったのです。

　そして、いったん問題が公になったあとも、日本人特有の曖昧な表現でマスコミや抗議団体に対応したりするものですから、さらに問題が複雑になってしまい、結局のところ日本企業は女性を差別しているという評判となってしまうのです。

If a foreign woman goes out drinking with male Japanese business associates, some will ask, "Why isn't a pretty girl like you married?" You don't have to look far into these men's minds to find a firmly fixed image about women. Most of them are just trying to build a good business relationship, but this kind of behavior is often found offensive by Western women visiting Japan on business.

The topic of sexual harassment has recently become an issue in Japan. Before being sent overseas, many Japanese men are now given guidance and cautioned about how to deal with foreign women in business situations. Some Japanese men living overseas are so sensitive and cautious toward women that they're considered downright unfriendly.

A number of Japanese companies in the US have been sued successfully by their female employees for discrimination against women. But when you look at many of such cases, it's important to see that the original cause of many of these suits arose with problems between American employees. Then, the problems surfaced, they were exacerbated when the company didn't take appropriate action. Such problems develop into lawsuits partly because Japanese management is unfamiliar with intra-company legal battles, and often fails to take steps prescribed by law toward solving sexual harassment problems.

When the problem becomes public, the situation gets even more complicated because Japanese companies respond to detractors and the media with typically vague expressions. They end up with a fixed reputation for discriminating against women whether or not they actually deserve it.

気をつけなければならないことは、マスコミの報道、あるいはマスコミによるインタビューの方法自体が、多分に自国の文化に基づくコミュニケーション・スタイルに依存しているということです。明快な弁明を良しとするアメリカのマスコミが、曖昧に和を保って回答をしようとする日本人と向き合えば、日本側の真意を取り違えて報道してしまうリスクがあるのは、いわば当然のことなのです。

It should also be noted that reporting style and media focus, related to each particular country's communication style, have a role to play. For example, the American media prefers concise, clear explanations. When reporters interview Japanese, the latter may answer in vague ways in an attempt to preserve harmony, and the Americans naturally misconstrue their real intentions and report the situation from that standpoint.

2 なぜ日本の女性はカワイコぶるの？

日本の女性の地位について考えるとき、欧米の人にとって腑に落ちないもう一つの現象があります。

とっくに大人として社会に出ている女性が、子供のような言葉遣いや振る舞いをしたり、アパートの中にぬいぐるみをかざっていたり、時には人前で泣き出したり。「日本の女性は本当に自立したいのでしょうか。家族や男性に頼って生きてゆく方が楽だと思ってあんな子供っぽい振る舞いをするのでしょうか。それにしても、子供っぽい女性を好きになる男性が多いということは、男性の女性観自体にも問題があるんじゃないですか」

あるアメリカ人のジャーナリストがこのようにコメントしたことがあります。

確かに、日本の女性の中には、敢えて社会で責任のある立場に置かれるよりも、現状のままで男性から大切にされて、金銭的にも困らない贅沢な暮らしを続ける方がましだと思っている人もいるようです。こうした考え方が、日本での女性の地位の向上に内側からブレーキをかけているのは残念なことです。

しかし、皮肉なことに日本の女性のパワーは私生活の上で男性と大きく逆転しています。例えば、日本で物を販売しようとするならば、女性の嗜好を無視するわけにはいかないということは、すでに説明をしたはずです。しかし、このことは、単に主婦が一家の財政を握っているということだけを意味しているわけではありません。男性自身が女性の好みによって自分のファッションを変えたり、ライフスタイルを変化させたりするからです。

それにしても、なぜ日本の男性はかわいらしく子供っぽい女性を求めるのでしょうか。巷に氾濫する漫画や広告のイメージをみても、女性の描写は独立心のある強い女性の

2 Why do Japanese women act so cute?

This is another aspect of women in Japan that Westerners have a hard time accepting.

Full-grown adult Japanese women sometimes speak and act like children. They often decorate their apartments with stuffed animals, or burst out into hysterics in public.

An American journalist once commented, "I wonder if Japanese women really want to be independent. Maybe they think it's easier to be dependent on their families or men and to act in such childish ways. And the Japanese male's view of women may be partly to blame, since many of them like childish women."

There are definitely some Japanese women who put a priority on pleasing men and prefer to live a luxurious life of ease rather than seeking a responsible position in society. It's unfortunate that in some cases the brakes are being applied from the inside to women's progress.

Ironically, Japanese women's power exponentially increases when it comes to home life. For example, the tastes and preferences of Japanese women cannot be ignored in terms of their impact on the consumer market. This means that housewives not only control the family finances, but they can also persuade men to change their clothes or lifestyles according to their preferences.

But why do Japanese men seem to want cute, child-like women? In the parade of advertisements and comics, these images stand out over images of strong,

美しさよりも、幼く愛くるしい子供のようなイメージを強調したものが目立つようです。

　この原因は日本の教育システムにあるのかもしれません。日本の子供は良い大学に入学するために必死で勉強をします。そんな子供を親も物心両面で支え、学校の成績を少しでもよくするために一家がみんなで協力します。

　しかも、戦後の裕福な時代に生まれ育った子供たちの多くは、ある意味では、学校の成績だけを気にした、過保護の子供たちといえます。そうした子供たちが今成長して、成人人口のほとんどをしめるようになっているのです。学校の勉強はよくでき、受験に勝ち抜いてきた子供の中には、子供っぽい精神状態から抜け切れない人が多くいるのです。この傾向は、特に男性に多く、そうした男性が自分たちよりも精神的に自立した女性よりも、子供っぽい女性を求めるのでしょう。

　というのも、今でも日本の多くの有力企業や中央官庁は、有名大学の卒業生を優先的に採用します。有力企業や中央官庁に就職する人の多くは男性ですし、最終的にこうした競争の勝者にはなり得なかったものの、こうした社会のエレベーターに乗ろうとして、受験戦争をかいくぐってきた男性が日本には数え切れないほどいるのです。

　日本では、画一的な受験戦争に対する批判が何十年にも亘って云々されています。しかし、誰も大改革を敢行できないのです。というのも、改革をしなければならない人たちが、そうした受験戦争の勝者なわけですから、自らの価値を否定するような改革を行うことが、なかなかできないのでしょう。

　かわいらしい女性が目立つ日本の社会の裏側には、こうした戦後の長い期間に亘って蓄積されてきた、世の中の矛盾が隠されているのです。

independent female beauty.

The source of such images may lie in the Japanese school system. In order to get into a good university, Japanese children must study extremely hard. Parents support these children materially and emotionally, and the entire family cooperates to help them improve their grades in school.

Children born and raised in this post-war era of prosperity were generally overprotected kids who focused on getting good grades. These children have now become the majority of the adult population. However, many kids who did well in school and survived "examination hell" to get into good universities remain emotionally immature as adults. This tendency is especially common among men, and they usually want a child-like woman rather than a woman who is more emotionally mature than they are.

Even now, most major Japanese companies and central government agencies prefer to hire graduates of famous universities. Most employees of powerful companies and central government agencies are comprised of such men, though there are countless other men who did not do so well in the "examination wars."

In Japan, debate about the examination wars has been going on for decades. As yet, no one has been able to overhaul the system. Those whose job it is to reform it are themselves products of it, so it is hard for them to implement reforms which negate their own values.

Such is the contradictory background of the Japanese penchant for cutesy women, which has its origins in the period of post-war prosperity.

③ なぜ日本人はあんなに受験勉強に夢中になるの?

　それでは、なぜ日本にはそうした受験戦争があるのでしょう。このことを知るためには、日本の教育制度と、その背景にある「お上」という考え方について触れなければなりません。

　特にアメリカと比較した場合、日本の教育制度は極めて中央集権的です。日本では全国津々浦々、学年毎に学習する内容も同じならば、教育方針についても、文部省の細かい指導があります。

　しかも、そうしたシステムの中、日本の子供は大学に入って専門分野の研究を始めるまで、誰もがあらゆる学科をくまなく勉強しなくてはならないのです。文学を勉強して新聞社や出版社に勤めたいと思っている人でも、数学や科学が優秀でなければ、有名な大学にはいれません。そして有名な大学にはいれないと、出版社に勤めるにしてもその選択の幅がせばまります。しかも、そこで勉強する数学は高等数学で、微分もあれば積分もあります。こうしたことが、学生に苦しい受験勉強を強いる原因となるのです。

　これに対して、アメリカの中央政府は、教育の問題をそれほどコントロールしようとはしません。教育のカリキュラムも地域によってかなり違い、教科書だって地方ごと、学校ごとに異なっています。授業のかなりの時間が、探究心をもつことや、自分の意見を表明する能力を引き出すことに割かれます。自らの興味に従って、その才能や能力をのばせるようになっているわけです。もちろんアメリカでもエリート学校に入学するのは望ましいこととされていますが、それでも仕事場でうまくやっていけるかどうかは、

3 Why are Japanese so fanatical about tests?

Why are there "examination wars" in Japan? The answer lies in the Japanese education system and the bureaucratic thought-process behind it.

Authority in the Japanese education system is very centralized, especially when compared to the US. The content of what is taught each year and grade levels are standardized throughout the entire country. Education policies are overseen and regulated in detail by the Ministry of Education.

Under this system, all Japanese children must study a full range of subjects until they enter college and begin specialized areas of study. Even young people who want to study literature and work for a newspaper or publishing house must do well in math and science, or they won't get into a famous university. And if they don't get into a well-known university, their choice of potential employers is limited. The math studied at higher levels is differential calculus and integral calculus, which forces students to study rigorously for exams.

In America, the federal government does not exercise nearly so much control over education. Curriculum varies significantly according to geographic area. Even textbooks differ depending on region and school district. Considerable class time is devoted to the cultivation of individual abilities to ask perceptive questions and express personal opinions. Children are commonly encouraged to develop their own talents and abilities. Entrance into elite schools is of course desirable, but

基本的にはその個人にかかっているというわけです。

　日本では、それに反して、全国一斉に共通した教育を受け、それをマスターし大学に入学した者だけに社会的に地位のあるポジションが約束されています。エリート学校の出身である人と、そうでない人とでは、完全に分けられてしまい、後者が前者に追いつくには、かなりの努力が必要とされるのです。こうしたことを考えれば、日本の教育制度がいかに日本社会そのものに、さらには企業文化の形成に、大きな影響を与えているかが容易に理解できるはずです。

　しかも、日本には文部省の定めた制度を無条件で良しとする風潮が根強く残っています。これが、日本に今尚残る「お上」という発想なのです。「お上」とは、権力構造の上部に位置する人や組織を指す言葉です。封建時代は、「お上」は絶対で、「お上」に反抗することは重罪をもって禁じられていました。封建国家から近代国家へと移行した後も、この「お上」の発想は受け継がれていったのです。

　というのも、近代国家を指導してきた政府の要人や官僚の多くは、封建時代に最も高い身分とされたサムライだった人たちで、彼らの強い指導力によって日本は近代国家として生まれ変わったからです。ですから古い身分制度を廃止した後も、彼らは政治の場を独占してゆきました。

　現在では、そうした古い身分制度からくる伝統は払拭され、日本は民主主義によって運営される国となりました。しかし、それでも「お上」を代表していた政府やそれを支えている官僚への盲目的な信頼と敬意の念は、つい最近まで日本の社会に脈々として受け継がれてきたのです。こうした信仰を、代表する例が、国家官僚の生産工場ともいえる、

advancement in the workplace is primarily dependent upon actual individual performance.

In Japan, by way of contrast, only those who have gotten the standard education, mastered it, and graduated from a good college have ready access to good jobs and elite status. There are separate tracks for those with elite educational backgrounds and those with more mediocre educational achievements, and the latter can only join the former by dint of extraordinary effort. So it is easy to understand how the Japanese education system exerts such a great influence on the shaping of Japanese society and corporate culture.

The unconditional acceptance of this system set by the Ministry of Education is deep-rooted. This is the idea of "*okami*," which still exists in Japan. "*Okami*" refers to the idea of the organization, or those at the top of the power structure. In the feudal period, opposition to the "*okami*" was strictly forbidden, and carried a stiff penalty. Even after Japan's transition from a feudal country to a modern one, "*okami*" remained.

What this means is that nearly all the influential government officers and ministers who guided Japan's modernization were former samurai—the highest status in the feudal age. Under their strong direction, Japan was reborn as a modern country. Even after the nation's class system was abolished, they monopolized the political stage.

Japan today is a democracy and no longer has a class system. However, the old tradition of "*okami*" persists, having been translated into a blind respect for and obedience to government ministry bureaucrats. A sign of Japan's continuing elitism can be seen in the prestige of Tokyo University—the former Imperial University—

東京大学への一般の人々のあこがれの中にも見てとれます。

　最近では、政府や官僚が国家利益のために機能しているといったイメージを傷つけるような様々なスキャンダルが暴かれ、政治的な混乱をも招いています。そんなことから、官僚的権威に対して疑問を持つ人が増えていることも事実ですが、それでも日本人は気付かないうちに、「お上」に従ってしまうことがよくあるのです。

　教育制度はその典型的な例でしょう。日本に中央集権的な教育システムが存在し、それを象徴する受験制度がある限り、いくら教育現場が個性を尊重した自由な気風を教育の中に導入しようとしても、そう簡単には変革ののろしを上げることはできないのです。

which is a veritable production factory of future bureaucrats.

Numerous scandals have recently tarnished the government ministries' carefully cultivated image of functioning for the country's best interests, above the muck and mire of politics. Increasing numbers of people have started to question bureaucratic authority, although they still usually end up docilely following the "*okami*"'s directives.

The education system is probably the most obvious example of this continued obedience to a system that has raised many doubts. As long as the centrally regulated education and exam system exist, real reform will not be possible—even if schools try to create a liberal atmosphere which values individuality.

なぜ日本人は英語ができないの?

　ところで、こうした教育制度のもたらした弊害の最も代表的な例が、日本の英語教育ではないでしょうか。日本の子供は中学に入学したときから、大学を卒業するまでの10年間に亘って英語教育をうけるのですが、それでも英会話のできない人が多くいます。なぜ、そうした現象が起きるのでしょうか。

　日本人が受験勉強の中で学ぶ英語は、その大部分が読み書きです。受験のとき、語学能力は、記述試験だけで評価されるのです。そして、受験戦争が加熱するに従って、山ほど問題が出され、それに回答できなければ大学に入学できないということになってしまったのです。そこで問われる問題の多くは、実際の英語でのコミュニケーションとは何ら関係のない、文法の細かい法則であったり、スペルの問題であったりします。

　もちろん、文法を正しく覚えることも、単語を間違いなくつづれることも大切かもしれません。しかし、日本の受験教育の中では、外国語を勉強する最も大切な目的である、コミュニケーションという部分が欠落しているのです。

　従って、日本人の多くは英語を勉強はしたのですが、しゃべれません。しかも、それだけではありません。受験勉強の究極の目的は、大学に入学することです。ということは、大学に入学して、その後社会にでれば、基本的には受験勉強は無用の長物となってしまうわけで、多くの人がそこで習った内容をどんどん忘れてしまうのです。

　さらに問題なのは、日本人は英語を学ぶとき、自国の文化や発想法で勉強しているということです。例えば充分なアイコンタクトもなく、相手と英語で話したり、曖昧な表現に終始することも、日本人の英語を分かりにくくしてい

4 Why can't Japanese speak English?

A representative example of the negative affects of this education system is the country's method of teaching English. Japanese children start learning English when they enter middle school, and continue until college graduation. Despite ten years of study, many people still can't handle spoken English. Why does this happen?

Most of the English learned studying for tests is through reading and writing. At test-taking time, language ability is evaluated solely through written methods. There are innumerable English language questions to answer in the heated examination wars. If you can't answer them, you can't get into college. Most of the questions have little relation to actual spoken English, but are detailed questions about grammatical principles, spelling, and so on.

Certainly knowing proper grammar and usage is an important aspect of learning a language. However, Japan's education system lacks an everyday communication component. This is ironic, since communication is the most important reason for learning a foreign language.

That's why most Japanese who have studied English can't speak it. Another reason is because the ultimate goal of test preparation is getting into college, and what is learned for examinations is mostly useless information. Most people quickly forget what they learned after entering college and becoming an adult member of society.

Another problem is that when Japanese learn English, they do through the lens of their own culture and their own ways of expression. Japanese who speak English are sometimes difficult to understand because

る大きな要因なのです。辞書に記されている意味ですら、時には日本流に解釈され、翻訳されていることがあるのです。これに加えて、受験勉強の中で、英語が歪曲されて学生に教えられている事実も強調したいと思います。

例えば、「I want you to go to Kyoto」という英語と同じ意味の文章を記せという問題の正解が、「You had better go to Kyoto」であったりといったように、英語のニュアンスの違いを無視したとんでもない問題が問題集にでていたりするのです。ここで記した、「You had better go to Kyoto」という表現は、実は大変高圧的で、脅迫めいたイメージを相手に与えるということを日本では指摘していないのです。

日本で英語を話す相手として一番退屈なのは、何と英語の先生だと言うアメリカ人がいます。英語教師は、受験英語のプロであって、外国人とコミュニケーションのできる人たちではないのです。そうした先生の多くが話す英語は、独創性に欠け、味もそっけもないもので、それこそまさに日本の受験英語の弊害を代表しているのです。

下手でもいいから、どんどんフレンドリーに話しかけてくる人を外国人は好みます。そのためにも、つまらない受験英語は忘れて、自然に自分を表現してみることです。どうすれば相手に受け入れられるかということを念頭に置いた訓練をもっとしてゆくべきではないでしょうか。

それでも、日本人は十分とはいえませんが、書いたり読んだりすることは比較的よくできます。従って、外国人の方には日本人と意思疎通をしたいときは、メモやイラストを利用することをお薦めします。そうすれば、最悪の場合は辞書を引いてでもコミュニケーションをすることができるのです。

they don't make enough eye contact, or they use ambiguous expressions. Furthermore, dictionary definitions and meanings are sometimes translated in a Japanese way. The main point is that the English used in college entrance examinations is unnatural.

Test answers ignore well-known English nuances. For example, the correct answer to the question: Write a phrase which has the same meaning as the Japanese expression, "I want you to go to Kyoto," is apparently "You had better go to Kyoto." In spoken English, however, the expression, "You had better go to Kyoto" conveys an urgency and a subtle sense of threat not in the original phrase.

In fact, some Americans feel that the most boring English is spoken by Japanese English teachers. These teachers excel at examination English but can't handle a real conversation. Their English lacks originality and spontaneity, and is another example of the negative impact of examinations.

Even if your English is not very good, foreigners appreciate it when you try to express yourself in an open and friendly way. So try to be natural, and forget that stilted examination English. Always try to focus on getting through to the other person.

Although I wouldn't say that reading and writing are in themselves sufficient, most Japanese can communicate to some extent in these ways. So foreigners can always try using memos and illustrations when they want to convey an important message to someone whose spoken English is in adequate. For their part, Japanese will probably be able to be understood, even in cases where they might have to rely on a dictionary.

5 なぜ日本ではあんなに堅苦しい名刺交換をするの?

　外国から日本にやってきた人が最初に不思議に思うの
が、名刺交換の風習でしょう。それは儀式めいていて、外
国人はどうすればよいか分からず、戸惑ってしまうはずで
す。

　いかに人と付き合い、敬意を表してゆくかといった儀礼
は、日本の古代の身分制度から受け継がれてきたものです。
名刺交換に代表されるような伝統に根ざした作法が、日本
にはたくさん残っており、この作法は多くの「型」を伴いま
す。名刺交換を例にとれば、お辞儀をするときの姿勢、名
刺を渡すタイミングと方法、その時に口にすべき言葉など、
すべては古来の儀式に起源を発する一種の「型」をもってい
るのです。大切なことは、その「型」をよく踏まえて人と接
する人こそ、社会の通念をよくわきまえた信用のおける人
だと思われることです。つまり、「型」こそはその人の内容
の善し悪しを示す、あるいはその人のプロとしての資質を
示すバロメーターとなっているのです。

　この「型」を学ぶプロセスは、学校教育の中にも見ること
ができます。小学校に入って漢字を勉強するとき、子供は
その筆順を徹底的に習得します。そのときに、生徒は誰も
別の順序で書いた方が書きやすいとは言いません。その通
りに書かないとテストでも良い点をもらえないのです。
「型」をマスターした者は先輩として、そして師として尊敬
され、学ぶ側はマスターの指導に従って、黙々とその型を
学んでいきます。

　子供が「型」の第一歩として漢字の筆順を学ぶように、社
会人は「型」の学習の第一歩として、名刺交換のマナーを教
え込まれるのです。また、会社によっては、名刺交換だけ
ではなく、人を接待するときの作法について詳しく記され

5 Why are Japanese so rigid about exchanging business cards?

The exchange of business cards is probably the first thing foreigners wonder about when they come to Japan. They often get flustered not knowing how to perform this ritual properly.

How people interact with each other and show respect is a form of manners carried over from Japan's ancient status system. There are many codes of polite behavior of the kind represented by business card exchange, and these codes follow a variety of styles. In exchanging business cards, there's the posture of bowing, the timing of when to give your card, and also what to say. These aspects are contained in one form ("*kata*") or business custom originating from ancient rituals. The proper execution of "*kata*" acts as a kind of barometer of that person's professional qualifications. People who use "*kata*" well are thought of as people who can be trusted to understand their roles and function well within society.

The process of learning "*kata*" actually begins at school. When children enter grade school, they study "*kanji*" and must learn the exact stroke order. If students don't write the characters in the set way, even if there are other easier ways to write them, they simply won't get a good grade on the test. Those who have mastered writing "*kata*" are revered as "*sempai*" or teacher, and those who are still learning follow their direction and guidance.

Just as writing Chinese characters in the proper stroke order is the first step in learning "*kata*" in childhood, the ritual of the business card exchange is the first step in learning "*kata*" as a member of adult society. So

たマニュアルを勉強しなければならないところもあります。

「型」は日本社会の隅々に見てとれます。例えば、日本のお店でものを買うと、店員さんがきれいに包装してくれますが、この包装も、ある種の「型」であるといえましょう。商品をきちんと包装するということは、それをいかに大切に扱い、かつそれが贈り物の場合、その商品がいかに心のこもったものかを象徴します。この包むという「型」を通して、日本人はその商品やお店の質を示し、贈る人の誠意までも伝えようとしているのです。「型」は単なる行為ではなく、行為を通して様々なメッセージを伝えているのです。ところで、その贈り物を受け取った人も、伝統的な「型」に従えば、アメリカのように、その人の前で贈り物を開けたりはしません。相手の誠意を尊重するように、丁重にお礼を述べて、その場では贈り物を横においてそのままにしておくのです。

　しかし「型」の学習が過度になれば、単に権威に盲従し、創造性や自由な発想が欠落した人間が育ってしまいそうで、そうした日本の教育制度や社会制度に対する批判が根強くあるのも事実です。

　ただ、「型」の中には、それを何度も繰り返すことによってはじめて、「ああ、そうか。そういうことだったんだ」と後で理解できることもかなりあるのです。伝統工芸や武道などにみられる「型」がそれで、長い年月に亘って習得することによってはじめて、人々はそれが実際の技能に深くかかわる重要な行為であることに気付くのです。こうした場合、日本人は長い時間をかけて「型」を習得する行為自体にも価値を見いだします。辛抱強く一つのことをやり遂げるという過程の中からから新しい境地を開いてゆけるのだ

companies teach new hires proper business card exchange, and new hires often have to study a detailed manual about the proper way to interact with people.

"*Kata*" are ubiquitous in Japanese society. When shopping, the store attendant neatly wraps your purchases. This careful wrapping is also a kind of "*kata*" to demonstrate how important the purchase is. If it's a gift, it shows that the gift comes from the heart. The quality of both goods and store is expressed by the "*kata*" of wrapping. It also conveys the sincerity of the giver. "*Kata*" are not simply meaningless actions, but a way of transmitting certain messages. Following traditional "*kata*," the recipient doesn't open the gift in the presence of the giver, as in America. Rather, the recipient expresses his or her appreciation politely and humbly, setting the gift aside in a show of respect.

However, Japan's rigid educational and social system has become the subject of much recent criticism. Some people worry that if too much emphasis is placed on learning "*kata*," society will merely produce people who blindly follow authority, and lack the creativity and the ability to think for themselves.

Yet many traditional Japanese craftspeople and martial arts practitioners have noticed that real skill occurs only after they have mastered the "*kata*" over time. Through repetition of these forms, there comes a moment of recognition: "Oh yes! That's how it's done!" There is value in mastering such styles through years of cultivation. Many Japanese see the acquisition of "*kata*" as a kind of spiritually rigorous training. If one can patiently work on a particular thing, a new world will

と、多くの日本人は思うのです。

　一見ナンセンスに見える「型」の習得のプロセスこそ、日本人の精神風土を形作る土台の一つとなっているわけです。

　加えて、こと日本に限らず、外国での人の行為の背景にある「型」を尊重することは、そこでビジネスを行う第一歩であるということを、ここで再度強調しておきましょう。

open in the course of that practice.

This process might not make much sense at first glance, but it is one of the foundations that have shaped the spiritual and emotional landscape of Japanese.

A first step in doing business with people from another country is to respect the "*kata*" behind their actions and behaviors. This applies to all countries, not just to Japan.

なぜ日本の社会は「平等」ではないの?

　80年代に日本経済が世界に向けて伸びていった頃、海外で日本式の経営が紹介され、社長から社員までが一丸となった日本企業のあり方が云々されたことがありました。

　ある日本企業では、社長といえども社員食堂でみんなと一緒に食事をしているとか、日本の会社には重役専用の駐車場がなく、誰でも早くやってきた者がそこに駐車するなどといったことが報道され、日本人は日本人で、我々こそアメリカなどよりもよほど平等を尊重しているぞと自慢したものでした。

　しかし、アメリカなど欧米での日本式経営ブームはそう長くは続きませんでした。そうした中で、「おかしいぞ、日本の企業で働いてみたが、思っていたような平等感覚はどこにもないじゃないか」と思った欧米人も多かったのではないでしょうか。

　実は、こうした行き違いの背景には、日本人と欧米人との間で「平等」に対する観念の違いがあるのです。アメリカ人は思います。「一生懸命働いて社長になったんなら、専用のレストランがあっても、専用駐車場があってもいいじゃないか」そうなんです。アメリカ人にとっては、チャンスがすべての人に開かれているということが平等であることの大原則なのです。そこでアメリカ人は思います。「若くても才能があれば、どんどんのしあがり、地位だって富だってつかみ取れる。それをつかみ取れば、それをどのように使うかは自分が決めることだ。それが自由ということなのだ」

　これとは対照的に、日本人は人を均等に取り扱うことを平等だと思っています。社長でも社員食堂で食事をしてい

6 **Why isn't Japanese society equal?**

When Japan's economy was growing and expanding in the 1980's, Japanese-style management became popular abroad. Many countries were intrigued by the way Japanese companies seemed to treat all employees relatively equally—from the president on down to the salaried worker.

Reports circulated that Japanese company presidents ate lunch with employees in company cafeterias, and that executives didn't have reserved parking but parked with everyone else on a first-come-first-served basis. Japanese bragged that they respected and valued equality even more than Americans.

But the Japanese-style management boom in America and Europe was short-lived. Western employees of Japanese companies observed, "Oddly enough, I tried working here and didn't find the equality I was expecting anywhere."

The source of such misunderstandings is that the Japanese concept of equality differs from the Western one. For example, Americans think, "If I've worked hard and become company president, what's wrong with using a special dining room or having reserved parking?" The main principle behind the American sense of equality is that everyone has the same opportunities available to them. Americans feel, "Even though I'm young, if I have talent, I'll be rapidly promoted and will achieve status and wealth. So once I get these things, I can use them how I want. That's what freedom is all about."

In contrast, Japanese view equality as the equal treatment of people. This is why they glorify the compa-

るということが美化されるのも、こうした平等観の現れでしょう。すでに何度となく説明してきましたように、日本の社会は上下の関係が極めて鮮明な社会です。そして、下から上に向かっての道を歩むときに要求されるのが、上の権威によって指導される「型」の学習です。このような状況下では、平等とはどのように存在しているのでしょうか。

日本での上下関係は常に人の心の中に根ざしたものです。年をとるに従って、その人の立場はだんだんと上に上がり、社会的な地位もついてゆきます。また年齢による上下に加えて、その人がどのような職業に就いているかといった社会的な状況、さらにはその人が顧客なのか売り手なのかといったようなその時点での立場などが縦糸や横糸となって、日本社会という織物が造られていきます。この縦糸と横糸とに従順であること。そして、すべての人がそれぞれの立場を受け入れ、そこでその立場を全うすること。これが日本人の平等観の根底にあることを知っておく必要があるようです。

すなわち、子供は子供として、新入社員は新入社員として、日本全国すべて同じ立場にあり、同じように行動し、同じように昇進してゆくのが日本流の平等なのかもしれません。従って、ある年齢に達したら「後進に道を譲って」、現場から退くことも、才能はあっても若いからということで昇進が拒絶されることもあるのです。たとえ若い人を昇進させるために、まだ能力のある人が早めに引退したり、給料が低いといったことがあっても、それは仕方のないことだととられるのです。

もちろん、すべての人にチャンスが開かれるべきとするアメリカでは、こうした年齢による昇進などはもってのほか、差別ともいえる行為とみなされてしまうのです。

ny president who eats in the cafeteria. As we've discussed, hierarchy is quite evident in Japanese society. What is demanded of you as you move up in the hierarchy is that you learn the "*kata*" or "ways" of being guided by superiors. So how can equality in the American sense exist in this environment?

Japanese are always conscious of differences in social position. As a person gets older, his position rises along with his social status. In addition to age, the social fabric of Japanese society is woven through with a consciousness of social positions, including the industry in which one works, or whether one is a customer or supplier. A certain submissiveness or obedience to the social fabric exists, insofar as everyone accepts his or her own position and strives to fulfill a designated role. The acceptance of social roles is deeply rooted in the Japanese notion of equality.

In other words, Japanese-style equality means that children act like children, and rookie employees act like rookie employees. Nationwide, everyone acts in accordance with his position and moves up within its confines. Therefore, equality could mean being denied a promotion due to your youth, even if you have the necessary talent to move up. It also means that after you reach a certain age you "bequeath the road to the successor." This leads to lower salaries or early retirement for older people, even if they are still capable, in order to let younger people move up in their place. In Japan, that's just the way it is.

Americans, who believe that opportunity should be available to everyone regardless of age, naturally find the Japanese practice of age-based promotions to border on discrimination.

なぜ日本は精神まで「島国」なの?

　四つの大きな島と、その周りにある3000余りの島々からなる日本。そう。確かに日本は島国です。しかし、地理的に日本が島国であるという以上に、日本は精神的にも島国であるといえましょう。

　アジアの東の端にあり、太平洋に面した日本は、その立地条件から様々な恩恵を受けてきました。日本は歴史上の記録でみる限り、日本という国ができて以来、他民族から侵略され、蹂躙されたことは一部の例外を除いてほとんどありませんでした。その結果、日本語という言語も変化することなく、必要に応じて諸外国からの新しい文化を導入しながら、安定した国家を造り、文化を創造することができました。

　しかし、そんな島国の日本は、自らが他の国にどのように映っているか気になってしようがありません。時には、外国に対してコンプレックスを抱いたり、優越感を持ったりと、常に他と比較しながら、自らの世論を形成しています。

　日本人自身、そうした国民性を認識しており、「島国根性」などといって、自らを皮肉ったりしています。「島国根性」とは、日本人が自らを蔑むときに使う言葉で、それは小さな島の中にいて、ひがみっぽく、外に対して常にぴりぴりとしている精神状態のことを示しています。小さな国であるために、日本は海外からの日本評に過剰に反応します。良きにしろ悪しきにしろ日本を他と区別しようとするのです。

　さて、現在の日本には今までにないほど大きな波が世界中から押し寄せてきています。ボーダーレス時代、グローバルな時代と呼ばれる現在、日本も他の国と同じように、

7 Why has insularity become ingrained in the Japanese character?

Japan is made up of four big islands and more than 3,000 smaller islands. It is certainly an island nation geographically. In many ways, it is also an island nation mentally and spiritually.

Japan is located in the far east of Asia facing the Pacific Ocean. It has received many benefits from this position. As far back as recorded history tells us, Japan was almost never invaded and conquered by other peoples once it became a nation. As a result, the Japanese language remained the country's national tongue and Japan was eventually able to build a stable and secure nation. It has created its own culture even as it adopted cultural elements from other nations as necessary.

Being an island country, Japan is particularly conscious of how it is seen by other nations. Japanese public opinion has been shaped in part by continuous comparison to others. As a result, Japan has an inferiority complex towards some countries and feelings of superiority towards others.

Japanese know they have this kind of national character, and use the paradoxical term "*shimaguni konjō*" (insularity) to express negative feelings about themselves. The term implies a certain envy toward and nervousness about the outside world. Because it is a small island country, Japan overreacts to judgments from abroad. Yet it sees itself as different from other countries and distinguishes its strengths and weaknesses by comparison.

Influences from the rest of the world are now pushing into Japan with ever greater force and frequency. In this borderless global age, Japan, too, is confronting an era

あたかも陸続きであるかのように世界と交流していかなければならない時代に直面しているのです。

　人々は活発に国境を越えるようになりました。ただしそれが、新たな紛争を呼び起こしているのも事実です。国境を越えて人が影響を与えあうとき、与える側も与えられる側も自らの利益やアイデンティティを守ろうとするからです。幸い日本が国内に血の流れるような紛争の火種を抱えることはないでしょう。しかし、日本も他の地域からの影響を強く受けるようになるに従って、それに慣れる過程の中で、あるいは不幸にしてそれを排除しようとする中で、国が右や左に揺れてゆくことは充分に予測されます。

　近年、豊かな収入を求めて、東南アジアや南アジア、あるいは中近東から数え切れない労働者が日本に流れ込んできました。また、国境を無視して流れ込む武器も、日本の社会を不安に陥れました。そして、以前にもまして、日本企業が世界に進出し、海外からも日本へ様々な商品が流れ込んでくる中で、国内市場を守るために規制すること自体がすでに不可能になってきているのです。これらの日本人が経験したことのない事態をどう消化してゆくかという問題をめぐって、日本の世論は複雑に反応し、差別問題や安全問題が議論され、日本をもっと開くべきだという意見と、封建時代のように日本人だけの安全な社会を守るべきだという意見とが対立しました。

　島国根性といって自らを皮肉ってばかりはいられない現実の問題を日本人は実感し始めているのです。

　そうです、日本の価値観と、世界の様々な価値観とが出会い、触れ合い、そして時には混ざったり排除しあったりして、発熱しようとしているのです。この発熱を、建設的

where it must interact with the world as if it were a country bordered by lands rather than surrounded by seas.

People are excited by the ability to cross borders. But it is bringing new conflicts with it. When people cross national borders and influence each other, both the side doing the influencing and the side being influenced try to preserve their own advantages and identities. Japan is fortunate not to have within its borders the flames of civil conflict. It is strongly influenced by other parts of the world, however, so while adjusting to or trying to repel outside influences, Japan will inevitably experience some upheavals.

Japan has become an affluent society in recent years. Many laborers have streamed into the country from south and southeast Asia, and from the Middle East. Japanese feel insecure and threatened by the potential exposure to military weapons which disregard national borders. Furthermore, as Japanese firms extend their operations worldwide, more foreign imports will inevitably flow into Japan. It is no longer feasible for Japan to restrict its internal markets to domestic producers only. Public opinion is divided over how to respond to these issues, since Japan has no experience to draw from. The problems of discrimination and security are the subject of debate, and the public is torn over whether Japan should further open itself to the outside world or preserve a purely Japanese society for security reasons, as it did during the feudal period.

Japanese realize that Japan is no longer really an island country, and that they can't hold onto the insularity.

Japan's values and the contrasting values of the outside world are meeting. Things are heating up in the process of this melding, and it remains to be seen

なエネルギー源にしてゆくか、それともすべてを燃やし灰にしてしまうのかと、日本も世界の他の国同様に問いかけられているのです。お互いの国の文化を知り、日本が自らの文化を再認識し、それを建設的に相手に伝え、相手も受け入れてゆくことが、今までのどの時代よりも必要とされているのが、これからの時代なのです。

whether this heat will be a source of constructive energy or whether only empty ashes will remain. Japan is being asked this question by many other nations, and more than ever before it must learn about other cultures and see its own culture in a new light. All sides must convey their cultures constructively and learn from each other.

誤解される日本人
The Inscrutable Japanese

1997年 7 月10日　第 1 刷発行

著　者　　賀川　洋

発行者　　野間佐和子

発行所　　講談社インターナショナル株式会社
　　　　　〒112　東京都文京区音羽1-17-14
　　　　　電話：03-3944-6493（編集）
　　　　　　　　03-3944-6492（営業）

印刷所　　大日本印刷株式会社

製本所　　株式会社 堅省堂